Alternatives to War

In a Time of Global Crisis

Spokesman Books

for the

Movement for the Abolition of War

Published in 2025 by Spokesman Books
publishing imprint of the Bertrand Russell Peace Foundation Ltd
for the Movement for the Abolition of War (abolishwar.net)

5 Churchill Park, Nottingham, NG4 2HF, England
www.spokesmanbooks.org

Cover image credit: Amber Clay

This text is the full Transcript of the 'Alternatives to War in a Time of Global Crisis' conference (September 2024) compiled from a recording made by Olivier Stockman of Sands Films and written up by Gill Hurle, Hilary Evans, Colin Archer, Sally Reynolds, Tim Devereux and David Collins of the Committee of the MAW.

ISBN: 9780851249483

A CIP Catalogue record is available from the British Library

Contents

Introduction

COLIN ARCHER, Vice-President of MAW

Colin Archer was Secretary General of the International Peace Bureau from 1990-2017. He is active with CND and Global Campaign on Military Spending (UK). He has been a MAW Vice-President since 2012.

It's wonderful to be in this extraordinary, unique place. And I think we're going to have a really interesting and, hopefully, important discussion today.

Sometimes people in the academic world talk about a 'wicked problem'. So let's think about war. I mean that's a really, really wicked problem, isn't it? Both in terms of its dreadful effects and the complexity of all of the issues around it. So, what I say is, when you have a wicked problem, you have to think hard. And when you have a *really* wicked problem, you have to think a lot harder! It's not just about mindless activism, it's really thinking out what makes a difference. What are the powers at play? Where can we influence? Where can we put our little piece of energy to make war disappear? And that's the challenge, if you like, for today.

On the train, I just happened to have with me a book by Prof. Johan Galtung. This one has the provocative title *The Fall of the US Empire – And Then What?*. Now, for those that don't know Johan Galtung, he sadly passed away a few months ago but he had a brilliant brain. A Norwegian social scientist who thought a lot about these questions – and in two particular ways. A lot of his writing relates to the first part of our programme. It's about the big picture. It's about geopolitics. It's about large principles like non-violence, for example. And these are the themes we're going to touch on in this morning's talks.

But Galtung also analysed specific conflict situations and thought a lot and worked a lot on them. He wasn't just an active conflict mediator. I think he possibly coined the term *conflict transformation* as a broader term to include prevention and post-conflict rebuilding, as well as conflict resolution itself. So I tip my hat to Galtung today, in memory of a man that some call the father of peace studies. He was a major, major figure and I think he would be delighted that we're having this discussion today.

One thing Galtung said was 'I don't focus a lot on disarmament and the arms trade and so forth. And you know why? Because if you have an embargo on someone and stop the arms flowing, they're going to make their own weapons anyway. They're going to find them somewhere. There are all these black markets and so on.'

He said 'Get to the nub of the problem, which is why are people fighting in the first place? What's it about? What are the irreconcilable differences that have driven these people to use weapons?' and I think that's quite wise. It doesn't mean that disarmament isn't important. We've all done a lot on disarmament, and MAW has in fact done many conferences and events around those themes. And more recently on the theme of weapons and war and the effect on the environment, both the emissions and also the opportunity costs of the spending that goes on the military instead of on the environment.

But today, we are looking at this central question of conflict transformation. And fortunately we have some great brains in the room: all of you, I hope!

I'll start with Paul Rogers. Some of you may have seen the little bios that were sent round or on the website. Paul is Professor Emeritus in Peace Studies at Bradford University, working there for 40 years – my goodness! But originally he was a biologist in life sciences and working in crop research in East Africa on environmental security. But I, as many of you will, have read his hundreds, if not thousands, of articles and interviews over the years. He's looked at the causes of war. He's looked at many aspects of the war system but also at the failing economic systems and the link between the military crisis and the economic crisis and equality and so on. Interestingly, he's lectured at the senior defence colleges in this country and is engaged with government ministries' evidence to Parliamentary committees. He is a past Chair of the British International Studies Association.

This man knows what he's talking about. Let's hear him!

The Insecurity Trap

PAUL ROGERS, President of MAW

Paul Rogers is Professor Emeritus of Peace Studies at Bradford University, working there for over forty years. He has worked on the causes of war, especially how they relate to global limits to growth, a failing economic system and military cultures often dominated by the need for control. He has lectured at Britain's senior defence colleges for forty years, engaged with government ministries, and given evidence to parliamentary committees. He is President of the Movement for the Abolition of War.

Oh, thanks very much indeed. And my response is, follow that!

Anyway, it's lovely to be here today.

I'm sorry, I can only be here for the first part – I'm going to have to dart out halfway through John's talk because I'm meant to be at another conference north of the river and escape.

The river gets in the way! Although I gather that the trip from Rotherhithe through to Whitechapel is very easy because it's on the overground - I hope it works.

What I want to try and do, if I may, is talk about the near future, mainly at the international level. I've got a short book being published next week, called *The Insecurity Trap**, and I'll quote from it a little bit. It tries to summarise the kind of stuff that I, and people like me, have been working on for a number of years. So it's very condensed but hopefully written for a general audience. Because I work mostly in the international field, its failing is seeing how it applies in the British scene, but Judith Large, who some of you may well know, has contributed both a foreword and an extra chapter, which broadens it out a lot. I think it will be rather more useful as a result.

What I'd like to do is to summarise, to follow on very much from what Colin has said, what are the really big long term issues and how they interrelate, and to argue that at least one of them is so pressurising us, so basically almost an emergency, that it may well have an effect, possibly a positive effect, on how we handle the wider situation.

So I'd like to look at three linked areas, and it's the linkages which I think are important; look at them in terms of problems, and then point the way to possible solutions and how things may have to change very quickly. The time-frame is between now and 2030, six years, something like that. And the main problems are essentially:

First, a militarized system, which is very difficult to handle and basically turn around. It has very strong pressures; it has immense power and influence right across the world.

The second is a failing global economic model because the neo-liberal system simply isn't working. We are getting absolutely obscene levels of super wealth these days, runaway wealth, and more people are being marginalised. You see developing in front of your eyes the potential for diverse revolts from the margins, and they take many different forms, including the rise of different sorts of populism. So that is not working.

And then the third thing, which is the real short-term killer, is of course climate breakdown. And that is a much better term to use than climate change. It is a matter of breakdown, which is now starting to happen.

Colin mentioned that I got into peace research through an interest in environmental security and taught environmental science for eight years back in the 1970s when the whole issue of limits to growth was starting to come through It was a very significant time to be trying to learn your way through it. Now, put all those together and we'll see the linkages. I think what we have to achieve is serious progress in the next seven to ten years on three areas:

Firstly, trying to move away from the levels of militarism; secondly, trying to start the process of getting a fairer economic system; and thirdly, urgently doing something, and something major, about climate breakdown.

And I think that, if we're succeeding at it, it may speed up the process for getting a wider transformation. I mean, to put the end before the beginning, I think we have a chance to do it. There are two possible routes forward. One is that we leave it so late that the changes that we have to make, particularly worldwide decarbonisation, happen so late that tens of millions of people may die in the process. The more positive route is if we really get our act together in the next few years, that may ease a lot, because of the capacity for rapid change when there's no alternative. It's quite remarkable how people can change when necessary.

So that's the framework. I'll go quickly through the military side, the economic side, and the environmental side. I'll try and keep strictly to the time.

On the military side, to take an example of what it's about: quite a long time ago, three years or so ago now, we had the start of the war in Ukraine. And in the first eighteen months of that, the share price of British Aerospace went up by 60%. The share price of Saab, the big Swedish arms manufacturer went up by 100%. And the share price of Rheinmetall, which is the biggest German arms company, went up by 200%. World spending went up by a discernible 3% in a year and in Europe it was about 15%. And that's just in the first year and a half of that war.

And a similar thing has happened since Gaza, because at the start of the Gaza War, almost exactly a year ago, there was a surge in spending right across the Middle East, and that has continued.

So the one thing I think one has to recognise, probably the most important thing on the military side, is that you could imagine, (just frame it for a moment), imagine that you have, from a position of one country, what you'll call a "good war" from that country's perspective, and possibly for all the people involved. What you want is a quick victory with very few people killed and injured, very little damage, and a transition afterwards to a rather more stable situation. That is the opposite of what is needed from an arms trade perspective. You've got to turn the whole thing on its head.

For an arms trader, and I use that term loosely – it can be in Britain, it can be in the United States, it can be in China, Russia, anywhere from the point of view of an arms trader – success comes from selling weapons. And what you want, in a decent war, from their perspective, is one which is, not only long term, but more or less everlasting. And what is really good for business is a violent stalemate. So neither side can win, neither side can lose, but they've got to commit more and more to trying to do it.

If you see it in a way which is happening today, Ukraine needs more longer range weapons from Britain and France to actually penetrate more deeply into Russia. And the Russians, of course, can reply to that. If they find themselves pressurised, they can start talking about using weapons of mass destruction. Whereas if Russia makes huge headway towards Ukraine, Ukraine will be certain that it will get much more support from NATO, because NATO has put so much into this that they cannot afford to let Ukraine fail. So in other words, neither side can win, neither side can lose. It has to end in negotiations and it's possible - there are some signs that there are talks going on behind the scenes, very tentative signs there. Maybe there will be a bit of a breakthrough during the lull in winter. But that's really being as positive as you can be. So you've got to look at this in a very different way from the way we normally look at it.

Military systems are also very focussed on national security. The people who are involved in them, whether they're the civil servants, the military, or the armed companies, the intelligence agencies or the rest, their purpose in the case of Britain, for example, is defence of the realm, keeping the country safe.

Now, if you turn around and say, "Well, the biggest threat by any level is climate breakdown", they say, "Well, you know, we'll do our best to prevent the consequences." And if you turn around and say, "Well, why can't you work with the politicians and make it clear to them this cannot be controlled, you have to prevent it happening in the first place?" they will tend to say, "Well, that's not really our role. Our role is to defend the country, not look ten years ahead at the new threats which we need to take action on now." And that's the point.

So essentially the whole military system is very powerful, and penetrates very far. One way of looking at it, I think Colin will know very well, the revamped and extended National Peace Museum opened in Bradford three weeks ago at Salts Mill. There is one peace museum in Britain, and there are at least 140 war museums, in fact, on some counts over 200, because every regiment has a museum and one tends to forget that the whole thing is warped the other way. So that's the first point.

The second point brings you to the nature of the economic problems worldwide. And again, this is a personal overview. We did in the 1970s, and particularly the 1980s, see a change in the world economic model. It started with Reagan and Thatcher and what was clearly the start of the neo-liberal period. That has continued, rather more disguised, but certainly there worldwide, and at root, to put it very crudely, it sees economic success coming much more from strong competition than from cooperation. That's at the root of it.

The Keynesian system has a rather more moderate influence, or it did, still does to some extent. But neoliberalism is very much in the mould of, "you must get people competing because that's how you make progress."

The problem is, if you're going to compete, there have to be losers as well as winners, and that is built into the system in all kinds of ways. It's become almost part of the culture. It was developed in theory in the 1940s and 1950s, particularly in the Mont Pelerin Society in Switzerland, meeting every year. Essentially it really wants small government, but the government is in final control. The system works by making sure there is strong competition and not very much of a safety net. You don't need safety nets because people have got to be encouraged to work harder. And the end result tends to be more wealth going into relatively smaller numbers of hands – an extraordinary level at present.

Sometimes, the one newspaper I take apart from the *Guardian* (my wife takes the *Morning Star*, which gives you an indication of the range of views in the household. Actually, it's not a very wide range, I might say) I take the Saturday *Financial Times* and there's a property section there, and occasionally I take a whole page and just keep it.

And one three weeks ago was just advertising, it was properties in London by one of the leading companies. It advertised seven properties on one full page, and the smallest price was a very cheap house just on the fringe of Chelsea, a flat rather, that was going for a mere £4 million. And then they ranged from £10 to £50 million. They were not all in Belgravia or Mayfair, they were spread more widely. And you get that every other week and far more adverts. In other words, there's a huge concentration of wealth, but there's also more and more marginalisation. It's not that worldwide people are getting poorer, by and large they're not. But the gap between a relatively small group of maybe 1%, and a rather larger, more successful group of 5 to 10%, and the rest, is actually widening. And that is a recipe for all kinds of anger and resentment.

Then you come to the third one – again, no detail on this – the whole climate issue, environmental limits. And you go right back to the original "The Limits to Growth" book**, which is very well worth reading. The people who were involved in that right at the start back in 1971 were quite astonishing. They were saying, "We are exceeding the capacity of the planet to handle human activity, and it's going to cause huge problems and breakdown." They didn't say next year, next decade, they predicted that around about the 2020s it would all go wrong. And if you look back on what they were saying would happen, they've been extraordinarily close to what is happening, because people have revisited the original and looked forward from that time. We are reaching the limits to which the world ecosystem can cope with human activity. And that is most commonly seen now in climate breakdown.

I've got a friend who's an applied meteorologist who's worked on this for many years, and he basically says, "Look, the climate science community are really very scared". He would use language like that because they see what is happening and it's happening much quicker than most people realize.

Now, if you put all those together, you think, "Well, we are going to have to give up, aren't we?" But that is not the case because if you turn around,

I want to just turn around a bit and look at it going backwards from the climate bit through to the others.

On the climate side, we now know much more with a fair degree of accuracy what is going to happen on current things. One of the ways you do that is you take the current models of what's going to happen and then you use data from 25 years ago and put that into the model and see what the model says would've happened, compare it with what actually happened and you get a pretty good indication of the model's accuracy. And the result is the accuracy is pretty good, but it still tends to underestimate the speed of acceleration. So they're very confident that this is happening. And where the climate science community (with a few exceptions), 20 years ago would be cautious in speaking in public because they feel they've got to have a united front, they will now speak out more commonly and more urgently than they did. So that's one thing.

The second thing is that public awareness is growing and people are more prepared to go to jail in support of trying to get a change. And also we're actually seeing the evidence of it happening in front of our eyes.

You look at that heat dome, which more or less destroyed a large town in western Canada in the space of a few hours (most people got out, fortunately), you see the floods that you've had very recently in a number of countries right around the world. The weather events aren't necessarily that more frequent, but they tend to be a lot more intense. And that is speeding up, so people know it's happening.

More politicians by and large will take very little notice of this, with one or two exceptions, because one of the troubles is, you have to act long before the problems really become critical. And by "long" I mean 5, 10, 15 years. The neo-liberal system responds when the market says so – and the market won't say so until it's too late. This is one of the fundamental problems on the economic side.

But what you are also seeing, and this is quite extraordinary, is there have been incredible developments on the ability to decarbonise an economy. The speed at which this has changed is startling. One of our sons is a renewable energy engineer, and another works partly on maritime sea wind farms. And Tom says, "Look, there's a heck of a lot happening and we know now much more how we can do it and how quickly we can do it." It is just, there's not the political will there to do it.

Britain could have been much farther down the line, if we'd carried on. The government through to 2010 was starting to get it right when they set up the National Climate Committee. But then it went downhill, particularly from 2015 onwards. And most of the really good developments were pulled back by the government at the time, the Conservative government, let's be honest about it. But you could turn that round again very quickly. It is possible to do this much quicker than people realise. And I suspect that that is likely to happen, but the real issue is, can it happen quickly enough?

Now go back to the other two. On the economic side, as some of you will be aware, there's a lot of good work going on, on how to create sustainable economies: New Economics Foundation and a whole cluster of think tanks and active groups in Britain. And that goes through to the rapid need for pretty wholesale tax reform, because the tax system, in terms of avoidance and evasion, and also in terms of the inadequacy of the whole system, is such that you're not getting the resources available that you need to spend. There is good work going on that, but it is still fairly early days.

What about the military side? The military side is the really difficult one. I think it's probably even more difficult than the economic side because it is a system which is so set in its ways. I've been very privileged: I've been able to do talks at the main defence colleges, the Joint Service College and the Royal College, on many occasions over the last 40 years. It started when they wanted somebody to talk about nuclear disarmament, because they thought they had to do that to tick the box. But after 1995, they started to want to look at, well, "What's happening worldwide? We'd be interested in other views". You never know whether this is window dressing, but at least you get the opportunity. When I went to the Joint Service College, they told me they had a pacifist from Cumbria who used to come and do a talk with them every year. So there is an opening there. I've been doing this for a long time and not holding back, except I really didn't hold back recently three years ago. I haven't been back since! But you never know. It may be just old age coming up.

The point about all of this is, it is possible to envisage change even there. I'll give you one example. You probably remember Richard Norton Taylor who was the *Guardian* security correspondent, still very active doing really good stuff on *Declassified UK*. (If you don't look at the *Declassified UK* website, you should do, because that is the one area where investigative journalism is doing very good work on a near daily basis.) Richard writes quite often there, and I was talking to him on the phone the other day about this new defence review and he said, "One thing that gets me, Paul, is that if you talk to some of the military, not the people who are in the public gaze, but behind the scenes, there are far more concerns, on things like the absolute stupidity of the Trident system, £200 billion minimum over the next 30 years. And it's unusable."

Like me, Richard holds the view we should have got rid of the aircraft carriers. Those two super-carriers are warping the whole maritime policies. Meanwhile, the Royal Fleet auxiliary, which can often double in terms of emergency relief, is under-resourced. So there's a heck of a lot, even within the military, people will think about this. It's not easy in their career progress and some of them tend to hold back till they retire. But it is not a complete edifice. And I think this is where one has to be prepared to be confident and push things very strongly.

I must be getting close to time because we want time for discussion. I said at the start that I think we are in a race against time. We have to make very big changes, ideally very quickly. If I give a personal view as we stand at present, I don't think it'll happen fast enough.

I think it will happen, because essentially when it becomes so obvious that we have to do something, which could be any time in the next five to six, seven years, then we eventually will start to do it at the pace required. But the issue is, can we do it quicker and more productively?

There is one definition of prophecy, which I rather like - one definition: "Prophecy is suggesting the possible." And all that means is that you are looking at what could be done, even demonstrating how people think it could be done, so that it is more common for people to think, "Yes, we could do that".

And then it becomes, "We have to do that because it is manifestly obvious that we can't go on the way that we're going on at the moment." I think that's very important for ordinary people, for academics and the rest who may have the resources to do this in a more detailed way. On that basis, you can look in a more positive way forward. I don't think it's going to be at all easy. At the same time, changes are happening quite rapidly. Surprisingly, (John might want to comment on this), it is clear that the Chinese – we don't yet know why they're doing it fully, I want to develop that – are producing wind and solar power at an incredible rate at the moment. And they make a lot of money sending it overseas as well.

So much could be done quickly given the political will, and the political will will come more when it's obvious something has to be done. It'll happen more if people are saying, "This is what you've got to do, you've got to do it soon." And don't forget that if you start to tackle the big one of climate breakdown, inevitably that throws light on what you do on the economic and indeed on the security side, because we've got to rethink security. It is not fit for purpose at present.

And this is why I think, there's room for optimism, and you probably heard me say this before, that if you work in this field, as I've done on nuclear and terrorism issues for God knows how long, you've got three choices: you're either alcoholic, suicidal, or optimistic.

And I prefer the optimism.

I don't always stick to it, but I think we do.

Let's leave it at that - plenty of time for discussion.

So that's it, I think we've got a few minutes for questions, any immediate comments or thoughts?

One right at the back first? Yes.

Questions to Paul Rogers

[RJ] Hi, Rebecca Johnson.

That was fascinating, Paul, as always. My question is about this so-called Security Defence Review because I can remember working so hard with the previous one, I remember you did.

[PR] Yeah.

[RJ] Get them to think about it as a security, as a strategic security and defence review because that's the way round. You can't determine what you're going to do in defence terms unless you actually understand what the security challenges are.

[PR] Yeah.

[RJ] Now we see this one put in the hands of Lord Robertson, (and we obviously know his past), very short-termist with parameters already set, so that anyone wishing to put in any kind of a submission, which by the way, the deadline is the end of September.

[PR] Yeah.

[RJ] But anyone wishing to has already been told you can't look at anything that is actually going to require long term analysis, long term thinking, long term decision making, or at least short to medium term decision making that will affect the long term. So could you, I imagine that you probably have a little bit more access at the moment than I do. I also was invited to teach for a number of years at Shrivenham.

[PR] Yeah, indeed.

[RJ] And then suddenly that ended.

[PR] Yeah.

[RJ] but how do we influence this government? They've got a big majority, but they're so frightened of looking into the long term at this point, and I understand why. But how do we get to, on these issues, influence them to recognize that if they actually want to budget appropriately for even the next five years of their term, that they need to look differently at security.
[PR] Yeah.
In terms of practical ways, I think there are three points to make.

The first is that Britain is very good at fighting wars, starting wars, fighting wars. We're one of the most war prone countries in the world, and we're very good at doing failing wars. And you have to remind people that we've had three terrible failures in the last 20 years, Afghanistan, Iraq, and Libya. The war against ISIS has never worked out. And essentially the Watson Institute at Brown University is saying 950,000 people killed directly, over 3 million killed indirectly, and 38 million people displaced in the wars that followed 9/11. And that basically, and we've been part of all those wars. So essentially we've done an extremely bad job of defending ourselves in the conventional way. So there's that.

The second point is, it is worth saying that defence industries are terribly inefficient and very profitable. They managed to make profits out of virtually anything. In terms of this review, I think one has to try and take it head on. You won't be listened to, but some people will. So for example, my view would be we should be aiming to take defence spending at 2.5% and basically cut it down by at least a third and put that money directly into key issues, and one of the most important is aiding the global south to change the nature of its economic developments energy wise, as quickly as possible. In other words, there has to be an emergency decarbonization. And that is far more important than big defence budgets because that is the biggest single security challenge. So I think you meet it head on and say, we're actually defending ourselves in the wrong way. And even just to make people think that say, we do not need Trident. It's unusable anyway, it's immoral, but we do not need it. It is just a delusion of post imperial grandeur. And basically you say, No, we certainly don't need these gigantic aircraft carriers, which are sitting ducks for modern weaponry. So I would say you've got to be, I hate to use the term in the current situation, the current audience, you've got to be a bit aggressive in a way and say, look, this is not going to work! And you've got to do more thinking. And maybe if one can start that move, I think, I know CND is doing something, starting to do this. I think they're thinking along the same lines. Wherever possible just look at it in a very different way.

[CA] Can we allow one more question or?
[PR] Yes. Well, if it's up to you.
[CA] We're over time already, but...
[PR] All right. Well go on then. I'll answer quickly.
[CA] Short question and short answer, please?
[PR] Yeah.
[Questioner] Very, very quick. Your view, thank you Paul, your view please, on the military industrial complex, the military systems you talked about, you see them really as pernicious, kind of going back to Eisenhower, calling them the military industrial complex and warning about them, you remember. Or just that they are, and we have to deal with them bit by bit. There's conspiracy theories - we see them as really wicked. acting together, leaning on governments and so on. Or do you see it more as part of a bigger system?
[PR] I think the difficulty is that most of them do not see it being wicked. Some may, but I think mostly not, and I think they don't really know what they're doing in terms of the long term effect. That's, I think, how I would answer it.
[Questioner] Thank you.
[PR] Right. Okay.
[CA] Thanks so much Paul. It's a pity we don't have another whole hour with you.
[PR] No! Thanks for even listening to me today!
[CA] Thank you.

* *The Insecurity Trap* is available from:
https://www.hawthornpress.com/books/changemaking/conflict-peace/the-insecurity-trap/

** A pdf of *The Limits to Growth* book is available here:
https://www.clubofrome.org/publication/the-limits-to-growth

Towards a World Voice Diplomacy

JOHN GITTINGS

John Gittings is the author of The Glorious Art of Peace: Paths to Peace in a New Age of War *(2018). He was East Asia editor and foreign leader writer for* The Guardian *from 1983-2003 and wrote extensively on China and on international issues. He was active in the early years of the anti-nuclear and Vietnam war campaigns, and writes a regular column for Oxford CND. He is a Vice-President of the Movement for the Abolition of War.*

(This is the draft text on which John based his talk at the MAW conference, 14 Sept. 2024 - not a transcription, except for the brief Q & A at the end.)

INTRODUCTION

If you search online for the phrase "world diplomacy" or "global diplomacy" you will find a multitude of entries all referring to the rules and conventions of diplomatic relations and intercourse with their origins in 17th century Europe, and to their practice today. ("World diplomacy", by the way, is also a very popular game which holds an annual international convention.) If you search for "world voice diplomacy" you will not find a single entry – at least unless or until I post a version of this talk I am giving now! But I think the meaning is clear enough: if I had to offer a definition it would be that world voice diplomacy is the diplomacy that gives a voice to concerns and priorities of global civil society – the "world majority". The task which we face and have always faced is how to link world voice diplomacy to world diplomacy, and under one name or another, or under no name at all, this has been the task of all who have campaigned over the past couple of centuries for peace and justice around the world.

[Toynbee, 1947] Our present Western outlook on history is an extraordinarily contradictory one. While our historical horizon has been expanding vastly in both the space dimension and the time dimension, our historical vision — what we actually do see, in contrast to what we now could see if we chose — has been contracting rapidly to the narrow field

of what a horse sees between its blinkers or what a U-boat commander sees through his periscope.

The narrow vision that Toynbee deplores is the approach of conventional world diplomacy, especially constricting in the cold war – he was writing at its outset. The "expanding horizon" is the one I am seeking to describe: the World Voice:

1. THREE STRANDS OF THE WORLD VOICE

a. The state-governments that are non-aligned, or at least only loosely connected, to the dominant world powers, grouped at different times in different organisations –

1955 The Bandung Conference, peaceful coexistence

1961 The Non-Aligned Movement, national independence, development, as well as peace

Regional groupings such as OAU and Arab League which on some issues and at some times act outside the dominant world power structure

We should take for granted the defects, sectional interests, internal power struggles within these groups. Their voice is defective but can be influential.

b. The independent voice of NGOs and campaign groups, arguably more coherent and effective than the voice of state-governments

c. The United Nations – in spite of denigration.

As a forum for world opinion – Sec-Gen at best, GA

As a multi-faceted working organisation — the specialised agencies; commissions and investigative bodies

Nb Three working together – eg in TPNW

2. TAKING THESE THREE ONE BY ONE

some historical observations

A . United Nations

As Erskine Childers, an outspoken defender of the UN, would put it:

> *The UN was born on a great tide of yearning among ordinary people for democratic multilateral institutions – institutions that would harness*

humanity's best intellectual and scientific resources to tackle problems which must never again result in such hideous conflict.

Next year will be the 80th anniversary of the founding of the United Nations, and the wording of the preamble to its Charter will often be quoted – or it should be. At least, the first three words that carry so much significance: "We, the Peoples…" What the preamble purported to convey was that the governments assembled in San Francisco had been mandated by the Peoples of the whole world to "save successive generations from the scourge of war", from the phenomenon of war "which twice in our lifetime has brought untold sorrow to mankind". This sentiment was part fiction, but it was also part reality, reflecting a sentiment that transcended national boundaries, after a war that had caused between 70 and 85 million deaths either through conflict or war-related famine or disease – some three percent of the world's population.

It was clear from the start that there would be tension between the principle of universality and the claim for a pre-eminent role by the great powers, and it did not take long before the great powers gained the advantage. However, the struggle of the delegates from outside the Big Five did achieve some results. The General Assembly won the right to discuss and make recommendations on anything within the scope of the UN Charter or 'relating to the powers and functions of its organs', except for matters actually before the Security Council: this meant that any issue that the Council failed or refused to take up could be discussed by the Assembly.

Both the Preamble and the first chapter of the Charter were also improved with better provisions on human rights and international justice, and on universal economic and social goals such as full employment, health, and non-discrimination. Here was the legal basis for the whole range of UN specialised agencies, health, refugees, children and many more, which we now take for granted and expect to act not on behalf of any power, great or small, but on behalf of the desires of the world community, on behalf, that is, of "We the Peoples".

B. The Non-Aligned Movement

At the government level it first found expression in the 1955 Bandung Conference – the Afro-Asian Conference. Unorganised at first, this then took shape after the 1961 Belgrade Conference in the form of the Non-Aligned Movement which continues to this day. Its weaknesses and its internal contradictions were only too visible and that is the aspect on which many historians focus their attention. But it did have some effect upon the leaders of the two world blocs even if they were reluctant to acknowledge it. It also provided cover and space for the other and more influential expression of the World Voice – the non-governmental movements, campaigns, pressure groups and formally constituted NGOs that spoke out for peace, development and justice.

Though it is often hard to assess the direct impact of the non-aligned voice at the government level, it constituted a force of a kind that both superpowers from the start in 1955 did their best to win over or to divide. The doctrine of "peaceful coexistence" asserted by the major non-aligned nations provided a viable formula for smaller nations seeking to avoid having to choose between one side or the other. After 1961 when the Non-Aligned movement acquired organisational shape, their influence began to count more especially in the UN General Assembly. Later that year, the nuclear weapon states gave ground, and agreed to an expansion of the Disarmament Committee, with new members coming for the first time from the post-colonial world. Then during the negotiations which led to Nuclear Non-Proliferation Treaty of 1971, the nuclear weapons states had to give ground again under non-aligned pressure. This led to inclusion of Article VI of the treaty: that vital provision that *parties to the Treaty should pursue negotiations in good faith "at any early date on effective measures regarding cessation of the nuclear arms race and disarmament".*

I am not going to follow the twists and turns that the non-aligned movement has pursued over the next decades, the set-backs and false definitions and re-alignments ...

But we can trace this all the way through to the concept today of the Global South which now has a larger and more effective identity than the formal institution of the NAM.

C. *The non-government voice of NGOs and other campaigning bodies*

One of the less remarked, but very significant, achievements of the San Francisco Conference was to provide the mechanism by which NGOs could have "consultative status" with the UN Economic and Social Council. Over the next decades, NGOs gained greater status and more rights to participate, sometimes against the wishes of the major powers. Over the years new mechanisms have been developed to bypass this opposition – for example to NGOs having a formal role in the General Assembly – by allowing them to participate in ad hoc hearings and to form separate relationships with UN agencies. By 2018 the number of NGOs associated with the UN had grown to more than 4,500. (This is just one-fifth of the total number of NGOs around the world). The author of one of the few studies of this phenomenon has called the NGOs influence at the UN the "conscience of the world". Their influence has probably been most profound in the field of the environment and climate change, but even when it is limited at the UN itself, NGOs can often influence policy by direct lobbying and pressure upon their individual governments. Of course not all NGOs express a truly independent voice and maybe regarded by others as partisan, indeed not really non-governmental, but in the round and over the difficult post-war decades, they have had an important positive role, whether outside or within the UN, which continues to grow. The world voice that I am trying to describe is not confined to formally constituted NGOs, and in the field of disarmament, it has historically found its outlet through national pressure groups and campaigns. These have had a very significant international impact at critical moments of the cold war. Though world leaders professed to be unmoved by the anti-nuclear movement, there is considerable evidence that they were swayed in private, and perhaps deterred by it at times from taking fatal steps. In the 1980s the efforts of the US Nuclear Weapons Freeze Campaign (Freeze), the European Nuclear Disarmament movement (END), and related European groups, began to cut through, increasing pressure on the Reagan administration to scale back its strategic nuclear build-up, and directly influencing the new Soviet leader Mikhail Gorbachev. The leading historian of this complex relationship between state elites and peace advocates, Lawrence Wittner, has concluded that "nuclear arms control and disarmament measures have resulted primarily from the efforts of a worldwide nuclear disarmament campaign, the biggest mass movement of modern history."

Taking stock: Up till now I have been painting a generally positive picture of the strength of the world voice that is too often downplayed, dismissed, or downright ignored. However, a positive view of our history should not become a rosy one, and we should not move to the opposite extreme and either exaggerate what has been achieved or minimise the challenge that we face, a challenge which is actually greater now than it was a couple of decades ago. There is no magic formula for peace: it may have a manifest logic to use the phrase of Jonathan Schell's – the *Logic of Peace* – but how can one convince those who prefer the illogical. World War One was a rebuttal to the conviction of peace activists such as Norman Angell who had sought to convince world leaders that war was an anachronism that destroyed economic prosperity, a persuasive argument that nevertheless did not persuade. Similarly, the anti-nuclear weapons movement has been seeking to convince world leaders for the past three-quarters of a century that the theory of "nuclear deterrence" which legitimises their nuclear arsenals is illogical as well as immoral, but in spite of the TPNW the Doomsday Clock is closer to midnight than ever.

So in my remaining time, I am not offering a blueprint, simply some tentative guidelines towards the more effective expression of the world voice, although we can have no idea how effective it may or may not be.

First, we need to reflect and amplify the role of the United Nations as a bridge between the voice of world civil society and the conduct of international diplomacy. Although all governments profess their adherence to the principles of the UN Charter, in practice they do so selectively, while the media is even more selective in its reporting. We need to remind and hold to account our government of its commitment to the Charter and of its obligation to support the UN's humanitarian agencies. Beyond this, we need to pressure our politicians and media to actually listen to what the UN is saying, and not only when it suits their purpose.

UN Secretary-General Antonio Guterres said last month (August 6th) in his message to the Hiroshima commemoration:

> "Nuclear weapons, and the threat of their use, are not confined to history books. They have once again appeared in the daily rhetoric of international relations. They represent a real and present danger that remains with us today. The message is clear. The lessons of Hiroshima, which once guided our collective efforts towards disarmament and peace, have been pushed aside."

His statement was not reported anywhere in the British media, just as the warnings he has been giving with increasing urgency on the nuclear threat, climate changes, and other dangers have been widely ignored.

Summit of the Future. This will be held in New York in two weeks' time, on the basis of a General Assembly resolution adopted without a vote two years ago. Two substantial documents have laid the groundwork, the Agenda for Peace in which the Secretary-General "offers a vision of a more peaceful, secure world", and Our Common Agenda, an earlier document from a year previously addressed the shared responsibility for sustainable development. The intention of the Summit is to endorse three more weighty statements: a Global Digital Compact, a Pact for the Future, and (to my mind most significant of all) a Declaration on Future Generations.

Second, we need to find more and better ways of connecting the lines between the multiple dangers that the world faces. Those who study existential risk, a new but developing field, can readily identify four such risks: the threat of nuclear extinction, the inability to halt climate change, the danger of a new and even more lethal pandemic, and the unpredictable consequences of AI. Of these four, the only one to attract the full attention of world governments at the moment is AI.

The study of existential risk has been criticised, from within the profession as well, as being too elite and divorced from political practice. It is geographically limited with most of the work being conducted in the US and Europe – ref, China. There is also a tendency to view it as akin to futurology, even to science fiction, although the impact of climate change in particular is bringing it nearer to home. We need to explore through it not just the science and technology of the existential risks, but the politics and social factors that underpin them.

Here we face the obvious obstacle of vested interests, economic in the case of the climate crisis, political and doctrinal in the case of the nuclear threat, and plain disregard in the case of preparing against a future pandemic. And in all these cases, we also face a deeper human instinct to avert one's gaze from the unpleasant, and to maintain an "optimism bias". Such optimism may be one of the characteristics of human behaviour which played a positive role in our evolution, but it becomes negative if it leads to blindness and refusal to face reality. Against this, there are huge efforts by civil society through campaigns and organisations to raise awareness of these multiple risks and hold governments to account. Efforts are being made to link these campaigns but we need to do much more to bring these forces together.

Third, we need to transform the way that our governments prioritise policy decisions. The top priority should be the interests of future generations: the current generation may survive, but the odds shorten for those who come after. The goal has already been set out in the UN General Assembly's 2015 resolution on "Transforming the World: the 2030 Agenda for Sustainable Development", calling for action to protect the planet from degradation in the interests of future as well as current generations. Such aspirations will only become reality if translated to the national level. The principle that all people are of equal moral worth should apply as much to future as to current generations, and political institutions and their policies should be "future-proofed" – the key word.

Wales: The Act defines long-term thinking as: "*The importance of balancing short-term needs with the need to safeguard the long-term needs, especially where things done to meet short term needs may have detrimental long-term effects.*"

Oxfordshire County Council April 2024 cabinet decision
The draft mission statement that Cabinet is asked to agree is: "We affirm the fundamental importance of meeting the needs of the present without compromising the ability of the future generations to meet their own needs. We will take a nationally leading role in putting intergenerational fairness at the heart of our decision-making."

The Declaration on Future Generations which I have already referred to includes the proposal to hold a five-year review on the issue and to appoint a UN Special Envoy for Future Generations. England needs to take similar action: the only attempt to do so far was by (Lord) John Bird in his Future Generations Bill in the House of Lords which was unsuccessful.

QUOTE TO CONCLUDE
[From UN Pact for the Future]

> *We are at a time of profound global transformation. Too many of our fellow human beings face avoidable suffering. We are confronted by a growing range of catastrophic and existential risks. If we do not change course, we risk tipping irreversibly into a future of persistent crisis and breakdown. Yet this is also a moment of hope and opportunity. Global transformation is a chance for renewal and progress grounded in our common humanity. Advances in knowledge, science, technology, and innovation, if properly and equitably managed, could deliver a breakthrough to a better and more sustainable future for all. We believe there is a path to a brighter future for all of humanity, including for the most vulnerable.*

Questions to John Gittings

Q: Well, if no one else, I do have one that I think is an area that's been missing in the discussion so far, which is this very serious problem of threats to democracy, populism, authoritarianism, semi fascistic regimes, the big man on every continent, everywhere you see them, these horrible leaders, you know, manipulating all the fears about the other and so on. I feel, you know, it's, it's, an absolutely major dimension that's not being touched. Any quick comments on that? I mean, it's a huge subject.

A: Well, one common trope comes to mind, which is that it has been argued that authoritarian regimes are better able to tackle the long term future than democracy. But actually when you look at it, it doesn't appear to be the case. Something I'm going into with my study of China, they're going to have elections every five years, at least. Not meaningful elections; sorry, anybody who's listening in Beijing. But there are other factors which mean that they still emphasise the short term probably more because they have to appease their populations by instant goodies. But I think I need to add a fourth point to develop what you've just said. Right.

Thank you very much, and thanks everyone.

Conflict transformation

DIANA FRANCIS

A peace activist since her teens, Diana Francis is a former President of the International Fellowship of Reconciliation, and current member of the Rethinking Security network council.

As an affiliate of Conciliation Resources, she worked for many organisations in supporting local peacemakers.

She has written many articles and several books and been a public speaker on gender, peace, power and transformation. She is a Vice-President of the Movement for the Abolition of War.

I'm an activist and I grew up a pacifist. My parents were COs [Conscientious Objectors]. I was an activist in the Fellowship of Reconciliation by the age of 15 and never looked back. So when I retired from doing international work for Conciliation Resources, that's what I do now, and it's satisfying and frustrating and all the rest.

In the International Fellowship of Reconciliation (IFOR), of which I became a branch representative and then a Steering Committee member, I met a lot of people who were working very hard on nonviolent conflict transformation. They were living in situations of extreme oppression, often poverty, being captured, tortured and all the rest. This was specifically in Latin America, which was very close to IFOR, and this to me was real peacemaking.

Reference has already been made to Johan Galtung. When he came along, which was later than the period I'm talking about, he came up with the idea of cultural, structural and direct violence. Anything that is harming people, oppressing people, doing damage to people is violence and we should call it by its true name.

I get very fed up when people call wars conflicts. Usually a conflict does no harm to anybody. You just get cross and then perhaps you learn something and then you move on. War is different and we should call things by their true names.

This work with IFOR was hugely powerful for me. What you have to do as a peacemaker is to support nonviolent transformation. I saw all these successes coming from actual nonviolent transformation. It had always been Martin Luther King and Gandhi. Well, they were dead by then but now we had these things going on in Latin America and they began to be successful.

We had the Filipino triumph in getting rid of President Marcos, the 'base communities' of the Catholic church mostly, actually with two people from IFOR, who were organised and had learned a lot. That was an amazing triumph!

And then, as that was ending, we had the beginning of the collapse of communism in Europe. So Eastern Europe went down. The Soviet Union broke up and this was fantastic. But as this happened, we began to see that something called conflict resolution, which we hadn't been thinking about, was also important.

I trained as a neighbourhood mediator because I thought my work was going to be back in the UK. I did eight years as President for IFOR and thought I'd finished – now I would be working at home. Then I got called back into international work. Well, one in particular: I worked a lot in the former Yugoslavia countries which were not a happy follow-on to the removal of Tito. Terrible things happened there and they had real live conflicts to deal with.

But in the former Soviet Union, what was happening was that people had lost their original identity, just perforce. They were Soviet citizens. This was all they'd been allowed; this is what they knew. Their own individual identities had been suppressed, and then those started coming out. And in the new freed units of the Soviet Union, there would be lots of conflicts arising. I remember going with Jonathan and other colleagues to the Caucasus region and being in a workshop where we got to a certain point in this conflict resolution type stuff when they said 'but what about the fact that we can't talk to these people? There's no chance we can talk to them.' So I thought, 'Ah, this is actually where I go back to nonviolent conflict transformation', and I worked with a colleague and we devised a kind of diagram which was called 'the Snake', and it went on being called the Snake for years. Eventually, it became Stages and Processes in Conflict Transformation, and that's what I'm just going to take you through quickly. (See diagram and notes, p 31)

So you start from the structural oppression and direct violence and all sorts of things going on at that stage; people really needing liberation, but who are absolutely powerless, completely crushed. So how do you get beyond that? It begins in small ways with consciousness-raising talk: learning to talk about what it is you are suffering and what it is you want to change, and really learning how to think powerfully about that yourself. And then you start building more and more of these groups. You make networks, you strengthen yourselves, and you get into the stage of mobilisation, group formation, empowerment, and ready for action.

It all looks wonderfully smooth with analysis and strategy and building support. It all looks good on paper or being projected on a screen, but obviously that's a huge thing and it's not static and you can have all sorts of push backs against what's happening to you. But in the progression of things, you may get to the point where you are powerful enough to confront non-violently the powers that be. And that becomes an open conflict. So you are really facing up to them and they're getting angry and scared, whatever they're doing. And you may be back to square one. You may be completely flattened in the process but this is the point you need to reach, somehow. in order to get conflict resolution.

Now, I can remember in the Arab Spring, various things were happening when people were being massively successful. But all too often it went back on what had happened. I'm a lifelong taker of *Peace News* (except they're in a horrid conflict now and I'm very fed up with them). But it was always 'for nonviolent revolution', and somehow I've gone off revolution.

I really like the word 'transformation' because transformation means through dialogue and this is dialogue all the way: dialogue, dialogue, dialogue. Through transformation, you reach a place where you have the basis for moving forward into the future. Dialogue is happening right up there [pointing to the early stages of the diagram]. You'll be persuading people to join your movement. You'll be building relationships between groups. You'll be forming coalitions. You'll be trying all the time to talk to government if you can, or the most powerful people you know. So dialogue's essential.

We're halfway through the diagram now.

Being in talks, with or without mediation, will need a lot of go-betweening. Think about Northern Ireland for instance and how long it took to get real dialogue to happen. That took years and years, but at last you got a real basis for dialogue. And it doesn't always need mediators. I think mediation has become such a thing, but if people can actually do their own talking to each other, that's even better.

And then you move into negotiation and that's when you move into the hard issues. And then, with luck, you can get to a settlement.

The rounded shapes [in the Snake diagram on the screen] are the stages and the boxes are the processes.

And if you've got a settlement in that time, you're building better relationships. You are modifying stereotypes. You can't talk to people in these ways and start thinking creatively without actually forgetting about being hostile and enemies. And you are beginning to process all the past hurt and damage that's gone on in the ghastly times of struggle and repression before that. So you hope, through that, that you can come to a point of reconciliation where people become friends with each other – and it happens. That's the good thing: it *can* happen. And from there, you are in a good position to go into peace building, rebuilding, community reconstruction, development, democracy, political participation.

It's a whole thing to build something worthwhile there, that will last and will need to be maintained. So one of the conditions of that is establishing and maintaining healthy power relationships. You have to keep always, always, always repairing, patching up, adjusting it. It won't be static. It has to be maintained.

So this last stage is a constant process of peace maintenance: constructive conflict management. There'll always be conflicts so you have to have conflict management to make sure they don't get out of hand. And these things are true in small ways. The whole of this could go on in a workplace or anywhere but it will never be static. It will always keep needing to be adjusted.

And that last phase is 'conflict [or violence] prevention'. You never want to go back to the violence. And the way you avoid that is by being always conscious of relationships, learning to look after relationships, learning to know when things are going wrong and not letting it get horrible.

The last bit I want to say is about the whole global situation that John was talking about. Everything is so terribly unjust and oppressive for so many people in the world. You've got all sorts of local horrible conflicts and wars, and you've got what amounts to the terrible north-south cruelty based on the past cruelty of colonialism. It's all pretty hideous and we have to start waking up and mobilising. We have to become educated and vocal. How do you make that happen? Not just for a few people but for a lot of people? So we have to up the conversation wherever we go, wherever we are talking to people. It's very difficult but we have to be in conversation. We have to educate each other and it has to happen globally. I don't know how we do it, but without it happening, I think we're sunk, frankly.

Sometimes I feel completely hopeless and I think we all feel hopeless, but act as if you're not. Certainly, if we just allow ourselves to give up, we have given up. But we are needed to keep going. (My little effort at the moment is to carry a sticker saying 'If war is the answer, it must be a very stupid question' on my backpack because that means you have good conversations with people on trains and so on.)

What we need is a very different sort of international relations set-up. It's pitiful at the moment. It's all about this gang (worst of all, *our* gang) against the rest, and picking fights. I was so astonished to see the conversation between president Xi and Blinken from the US. Oh no, they mustn't talk! He shouldn't have done that! Was it Trump who was shouting about that? (The less attention we pay to that person, the better). Even Kamala Harris wants to keep up in the military. Keir Starmer, Kamala Harris – they all want to keep the weapons, build the weapons and have more and more military spending.

Somehow, we have to get ourselves out there, endlessly going through these processes with people. We have to build a movement that's as powerful as can be. If we can stay way up there, we may even start making progress.

Questions to Diana Francis

Q: Have you got a general comment on why you think sometimes it all goes very well and sometimes it doesn't?

A: I could make one up, but I mean, what I can think of is there's probably quite a long history to some of the things that work. I think very sudden things are very precarious. So thinking back (I can't in detail, it's so long ago), but the Latin American struggles, they went on and on and on and people disappeared and people were tortured and they went on, they persisted and they persisted. And then at last, I suspect they built enough popular support that actually the bullies didn't have enough backing to carry on. I can't tell you, I should think there are all sorts of things of chance as well, you know, which way the wind blows (almost) this morning. I think it's very difficult, but when it comes together, I'm trying to think back to Marcos and how he was overthrown. There was already a civil war almost, wasn't there? And that's when they came out and the nuns sat in front of the army and the one army switched and he had to scarper. So I think you just have to do it - as if. Thank you, sorry.

Q: Thank you so much for your talk, really inspiring. I'm really interested in your experience of community mediation and international peacekeeping. And I was interested to hear you say that this model kind of applies to both. And I was wondering if you could say a few words about the challenges of applying something which works in a sort of local community mediation setting to kind of the challenges of international diplomacy and peace-making at a national scale. Sometimes, you know, moving different scales can be so different. Yes. So I just wonder if you could say something about that.

A: Well, I think, a couple of things that come to mind quickly: that needs to be quick because the people, if you haven't got big power and responsibility on your back, you can move. So if it's just two neighbours, they don't have to show anybody else that they're in charge or humiliate themselves by giving up on a long held position. They can just say, oh yeah, if, if you stop banging away upstairs in an unpleasant manner, I could stop slamming the door in your face or something. I mean, they're fairly simple things and it's just a toxic relationship that's spilled up. Whereas when it's people at the top and it's very complex and long standing, there are so many, so many slips that could happen. And, and then some people will remain entrenched and don't want to be human.

Q: Thank you. Uh, thank you for that insightful presentation. Actually, I admire the model and the emphasis on dialogue. So I'm actually from Sri Lanka and I have been in conflict situations. Yes. And something that I would like to reflect is that, when it comes to the concept of dialogue, I believe in the importance of training and awareness in nonviolent communication because we try to bring the communities within the communities. We will have the perpetrators, we have the victims, we have the change makers. So I think it's important that we kind of give importance to the training of nonviolent communication.

A: Very good. And some form of leadership that is coming from within the community.

Q: Yeah. Which I believe in servant leadership. We need to have that sense of servant leadership, and nonviolent communication coming from the communities. Yeah. So I would like to ask, what do you think about my proposal?

A: I think, I think it's absolutely excellent, really. And, and if we have conflicts all the time, even in the peace movement, I think that sort of practice is absolutely excellent. And if you're going to be effective in any of this sort of work, it's no good having dialogue if you're going to call each other names. You need respect, always respect. And to me, I think human kindness as well.

Q: Could I ask (this is fascinating), about the politics, which can lie behind conflict? In other words, I understand conflict optimism, a result of

misunderstanding and hostility and antagonism and so on, and you want to get rid of all that, but behind that or beyond that, there may be irreducible political differences. Are you able to tackle those as well?
A. Oh me, you mean could it possibly be tackled?
*Q: I mean any, any anybody engaged in conflic*t
A: It's a major problem, obviously - I mean, identity conflicts.
Q: I was referring to those tribal people.
A: They had their land, first of all, stolen by the British and then handed over to be incorporated by a national government when it got its independence - although they declared that they did not want to be part of that country; they wanted to go back to being their own people. That resentment will take generations to go. I suspect the younger people now are getting fed up with it, but you've got these factions who have come into, you know, ideological difference, new factions, new fights between the leaders, new factions. There were the two armed resistance factions, which fighting and killing each other. The killing eventually stopped, thanks to local reconcilers, but the number of factions has now grown and they rob the general population by so-called taxation.

So it is difficult and I think profound ideological differences must be very difficult to get past. But you've got to have a degree of human understanding that can get underneath those things. And it can happen that you forget that you, well it's like I can talk to, I mean you can have friendships with people you profoundly disagree with and if you've got that, you have got some basis for solving things.
Q: I wanted to ask Diana if you have a guide to useful resources on your topic area or if not, whether MAW could assist in getting one together. And my motive for asking that is that my feeling is that if we are to raise popular consciousness and gain more popular support for our ultimate aim globally, we do need to show that we can support with local conflicts. And by that I mean much more than a neighbour dispute.
There's obviously a huge need for your sort of interventions and I'm wondering whether you are aware of a number of networks like your own, that could act, that actually produce useful materials and that could actually intervene in these situations.
A: I think it's, it's materials and people building the confidence to deal with those situations and there, there are a lot of neighbourhood mediation schemes and some of those have developed into being … I know, I used to work for Bristol Mediation and they now do larger things as well as just, you know, people arguing about noise and dog poo and so on. So, those are

there. But Jonathan, you were going to say something. I mean, there's a lot of literature and there isn't that much that's linking the community level to the international level. But the sort of work that Dan has been talking about, if you wanted to start somewhere, there's a fantastic book by Tom Woodhouse, Oliver Ramsbotham and Hugh Miall called Contemporary Conflict Resolution'. It's the contemporary "Bible" on conflict resolution. It's just a very good primer overview written by people, three people with an awful lot of experience. I actually wrote a book which is called *People*, it was my PhD book. So it's got a few detailed examples of workshops and negotiation things, because that's what I had to produce was this detail and it's anonymized and so on.

Q: I was hoping you might say something about gender as one of your topics. Have you time for a few words on that?

A: I suppose when I first went into doing international work, I was actually asked sometimes, because there weren't many women doing it but that's changed now. I worked in a couple of… my best one was I had to do a kind of self-transformation thing for one of the paramilitaries in Northern Ireland. I thought I was doing it with somebody else, but it was just me. It was me and a Brigadier and 10 'Brigadier sidekicks'. And they'd all been imprisoned on life sentences and they'd all just been released and they'd been given the job of disarming their people. They had disarmed very quickly. They got a very short deadline and they were so nice and so vulnerable, really. They'd done all this time in jail. They said, we wasted time on metal work while the Shinners were getting themselves degrees. And 'the Shinners' [Sinn Fein men], of course now you see them driving in big cars and here we are and we've got to do this and how do we go about it? It was really very touching and very sad. And, um, one of them said, 'You know, what would my father think - that I'm thinking of disarming?' He was a bit drunk and he told me about all these terrible things his father had done,' and now I'm kind of giving up'. And I said, well, but you'll do it. You know, you've made up your mind. Come on. And he said, 'Well, this leg wants to go forward, but this leg just, just doesn't want to go'. And it's hard for them. And I think, in the end, people are people and being aware of that and being prepared for finding vulnerability and feeling your own, I think it can be very powerful.

Colin Archer: Okay. I think we have to close it there. Thank you Diana, wonderful talk and I think really a very good introduction to the afternoon sessions.

DIANA FRANCIS - STAGES & PROCESSES IN CONFLICT

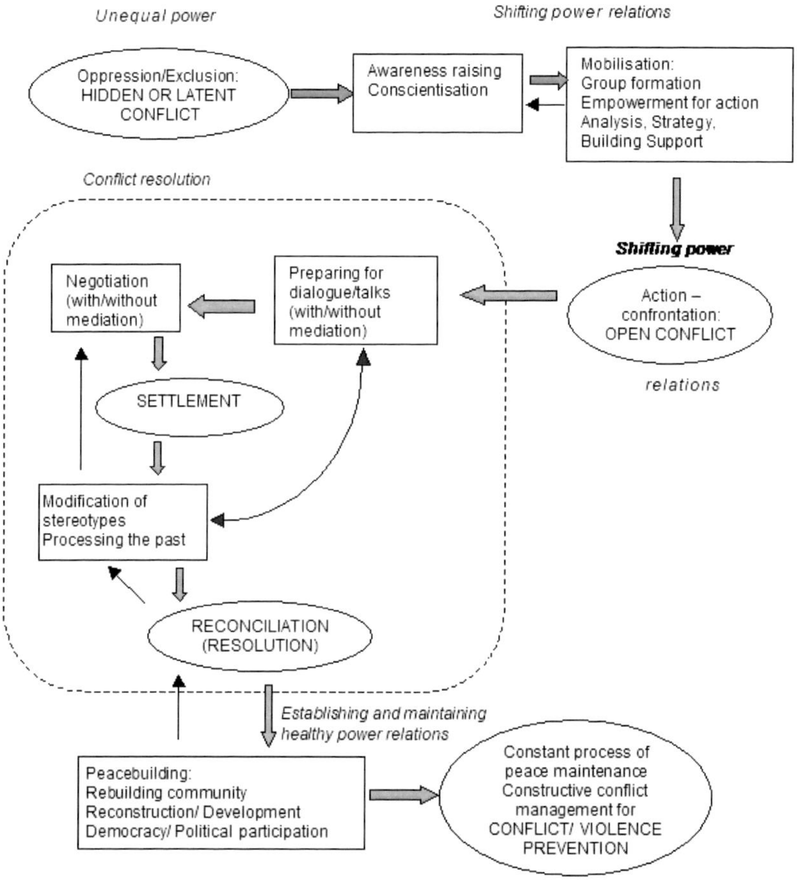

This diagram aims to show the stages and processes that will typically need to be passed through, if a situation of oppression, with an extreme imbalance of power, is to be transformed into one of genuine peace. (The words contained in the oval shapes describe conflict stages, while those contained in rectangles describe the actions or processes by which new stages are reached.)

Such diagrams do not present reality but ideas about it, and should be seen simply as tools for thinking and discussion. In practice, the 'stages' represented in this one are not in themselves static; they have their own dynamics and in reality may merge with one another. Neither are they likely to follow each other in a clear and orderly sequence. It will often be a case of 'two steps forward and one step back', or even vice versa; and frequently processes need to be repeated, built on, reinforced by other processes, in order to bring about substantial progress. And the ideal of conflict transformation is often no more than that, at the stage of confrontation. This reality is reflected in the diagram's later stages, which are largely about recovery from violence.

In addition, large-scale conflicts are not simple or single affairs, but usually involve multiplicities of issues, parties and sub-parties. They will, in all likelihood, also involve conflicts and power struggles within as well as between parties, and the stages of these internal conflicts will not coincide with the stage the overall conflict has reached.

The diagram begins with a situation in which the oppression (or exclusion) is so complete that the conflict is hidden or latent, the oppressed group remaining passive in the face of extreme injustice or structural violence (often maintained by physical violence, or the threat of it). They may remain passive because of tradition, or lack of awareness, or because the power imbalance is such that they have no chance of being taken seriously in any demands or requests they might make. In order for this to change, some individual or group will need to begin to reflect upon, understand and articulate what is happening, and encourage others to do the same: a process described in the liberation language of Latin America as 'conscientisation'.

This process will, if it generates sufficient determination, lead to the formation of groups committed to change. Their first task will be to continue the process of reflection and analysis, formulating a common purpose and strategy, then developing organisationally as they begin to take action to build support and so increase their relative power.

Some oppressed groups choose to use violence in their struggle. For others violence is not something to consider, or is not seen as a practical option. For yet others it is a matter of clear strategic choice or principle to act nonviolently. The term 'conflict transformation' implies the nonviolent option.

As their power and visibility increases, as their voice begins to be heard, these groups will increasingly be seen as a threat by those in power, and a stage of open confrontation becomes inevitable – a stage which may well involve repressive measures, including physical violence, on the part of the oppressive power holders, even if the oppressed group have opted to act nonviolently. (Sometimes at this point nonviolent resistance will turn to violence.) During this stage of open conflict, the relationship in power between the opposing parties will change, as a result of their ongoing confrontation, and other developments may take place within the parties or in the wider environment.

Even if the confrontation takes the form of armed conflict, eventually a road back to dialogue has to be found. Once the oppressed group have increased their relative power or leverage sufficiently, they can expect to be taken seriously as partners in dialogue. At this stage it is possible to begin the processes grouped together and described as 'conflict resolution', in which communications are somehow restored and settlements reached.

This will not be a smooth process: talks may break down, agreements may be broken, the conflict may flare up again. Non-partisan intervention can help, for instance in the form of mediation, both in preparing the parties for negotiation and in the negotiations themselves. And through the work of preparing the ground, and through face to face dialogue, some of the heat may be taken out of the situation, some more hope and trust generated, some of the prejudice dissipated; which in turn will facilitate the reaching of and adherence to agreements. Once these are in place, it may be possible to begin to deal with some of the remaining psychological damage which the conflict and its causes have occasioned, and to develop more positive relationships between the previously conflicting groups.

These more positive relationships will be consolidated through a long-term process of peace-building, and will find expression in social, political and economic institutions. But societies never remain static, and the final phase of 'peace' will need to be, in fact, a process (made up of a thousand processes) of maintaining awareness, of education, management of differences, and adjustment and engagement at all levels, so that some new situation of oppression – or other major source of conflict – does not develop, and just and peaceful relationships are maintained.

Note: Extreme imbalances of power are not the only starting point for the route to open conflict. The stages and processes leading to it may begin elsewhere. But questions of power and justice need to be taken into account in any consideration of conflict and how to engage in or respond to it. On the one hand, the untimely 'resolution' of conflict may mean in practice the suppression of just aspirations: 'pacification' rather than 'peacemaking'; on the other hand, those wishing to enter into conflict in the name of a just cause need to do so with some understanding of the likely cost to all concerned, and of their current and future possibilities, in the light of the distribution of power.

The work of Conciliation Resources

JONATHAN COHEN

Jonathan Cohen is Executive Director of Conciliation Resources, and has supported dialogue and peacebuilding initiatives in contexts including the South Caucasus, Kashmir, the Philippines, Colombia, Ethiopia, Nigeria and Papua New Guinea. He is an Associate of the Institute for the Public Understanding of War and Conflict at the Imperial War Museum and a Board Member of the Peace Dividend Initiative. From 2018-2024 he was Chair of the European Peacebuilding Liaison Office, a network of 50 peacebuilding organisations.

Thank you for the morning sessions, which I thought were really thought provoking and inspiring.

I'm going to talk a bit about Conciliation Resources and our approach to addressing issues of violent conflict around the world, in this first session. And I'll be talking later on about a particular case study, the Philippines, because, sadly, a colleague of mine, who was due to come, couldn't come.

What I want to reflect on to start with is a little bit about going from this broad discussion of some of the global challenges and then some of the approaches and methodologies that we've heard. What does it mean to turn these ideas into the practice of being part of an organisation that has a mission to try and transform violent conflict and to try and make peace processes work better and to make peace possible? And it's very clear that we're doing this at a time when global conflict feels like it's on overdrive. We live in a world where there are currently more than 120 million people displaced. I can remember giving a talk, some five or six years ago, talking about there being 65 million people displaced – the same as the population of the UK. And within the space of less than half a decade, we've seen that number more or less double.

So that just, without rolling off any other statistics, and one could give endless statistics of how grim it is - that's a level of the gravity of change, of escalation of conflict we see around the world, and it's a world in which some of the notions when I started out in this field 30 years ago, used to think of trying to attain comprehensive peace agreements to bring to an end violent conflicts. And there are very few comprehensive peace agreements these days and conflicts seem to be much more fragmented.

And there's a lot more focus on how do you address fragmented conflicts in localised peace agreements that might build up to peace agreements that address a more systemic dimension of conflict and, thinking beyond the notions of the big man mediator and sort of linear peace processes that lead to the signing of an agreement.

We are in a very different environment and a very different world, and we're looking at mediation and peace building in a different light. We are looking at the way it works at community levels linking to political levels and how the two influence one another. We recognise that political leaders and political elites might play an essential role in the signing of peace agreements, but this is never sufficient to sustain peace. What does it mean to build a peace that is sustainable and one that is more inclusive of the multiple aspirations in a society? How can those aspirations shape what agreements might look like? These are some of the questions that we ask ourselves in the work that we do as an organisation that is focused on peacebuilding and focused on making a process of peace more effective.

I think it's really important in thinking about this to also think about who is it that builds peace. We are a peacebuilding organisation with our headquarters in London, but we've evolved in the last five or 10 years enormously from being an organisation in which 90% of our staff worked out of London to one where we have almost 50/50 split between staff in the UK and staff in the contexts where we work, and the staff in the contexts where we work primarily are people from those contexts, and rooted in those contexts. As we've changed as an organisation, the people who build peace are people within their own societies.

When we set up Conciliation Resources 30 years ago, my colleagues who founded the organisation had a mantra, and this is partly how we got the name we had, which always amuses a lot of people, including many of our staff, the people who are most affected by violent conflict, most often the people who have the most nuanced understanding of what needs to be done about that conflict, but the fewest resources to do anything about it.

So how do you resource people who are affected by violence to transform their conflict, to build peace? We accompany them in that process. We can build relationships with them that can enable us to challenge them to think differently, but they are the people who have to be the primary agents and they're the people who own the conflict. And that's not easy because we must also avoid fetishizing the local. Conflicts happen for a multiplicity of reasons. Some of those are geopolitical, many of those are economic, but they are also because of dynamics within societies and the local will often generate the conflict. So there's a very complex dynamic in how conflicts happen, how they're sustained and who it is who can play a role in building that peace.

And it is an ecosystem. At the heart of good peacebuilding, conflict resolution, conflict management, conflict transformation has to be rigorous analysis, providing a deep seated understanding of why conflicts happen, and then using that as a basis to understand what can change a situation in order to move towards a sustainable peace.

Our experience at Conciliation Resources has very much been about trying to understand the power dynamics and the snake diagram that Diana has shown earlier is something that implicitly informs our work, recognizing that it's not a linear process. The snake charts a path, but there are lots of arrows in that snake that take you back because conflicts ebb and flow.

One of the answers – John was sitting here earlier and asked this question – one of the answers about the dynamics of conflicts and is it possible to change things – is I think it's often about being able to seize the moment because the tectonic plates of a conflict will always shift at moments you don't anticipate.

And a lot of the work of peacebuilding is trying to support people to be ready to seize opportunities when the tectonic plates of a conflict shift. The so-called Arab Spring, is a painful example of that because communities brought the energy of change, but they weren't fully ready to deal with the consequences of that change. And then when you had outside actors coming in, it created a terrible mess and the region continues to live with that mess.

One of the things that is really important is you have to engage for the long term. You can't parachute in, disappear, come back later. You need to work in accompaniment with people over a long period of time. Conflicts are generational. They take a long time to address and to transform.

At the heart of this, from our perspective as an outside actor is: what does it mean to work in partnership with people inside a context? What does it mean to support their endeavours over the long term to help resource those endeavours? Recognizing that there is a fundamental inequality in the relationships or a variety of reasons, for instance language can matter - it can be a real advantage to be able to work in English because it can get you through the door more easily with governments and donors. There is an inequality in this but it can be used to the advantage of partners.

One of the things we have to learn to do is how do we actually open the door for the people who are most affected to get into the spaces to advocate for change. So partnership is about reflecting on the relationship you have with the people in context and, and how you help them to bring about change and to change the roles that you have.

I want to share a few thoughts and examples about some of what it is that we bring to peace processes in working with people who are most affected. I've got, I think, half a dozen themes and examples that I'll share and try and hopefully not throw in examples from too many places. But when I talk about the Philippines later on, I'll dig deeper into one particular example.

One of the things that we found is valuable for people who are affected by the scourge of violent conflict is to know that what they're doing is not unique – they are building on the experience of lots of other people.

I started my professional and intellectual journey in this field in the Caucasus. And I was a Russianist many years ago. And I often think of the opening lines of *Anna Karenina*, where Tolstoy talks about all happy families being happy in the same way, and all unhappy families are unhappy in their own particular way. And in a way, I think that's what societies enduring conflict are: they endure conflict in their own particular way, but it doesn't mean they can't learn from the experience of other people.

One of the things that's fundamental for our organisation is the whole issue of what does it mean to learn from other context and how can we as an organisation help our colleagues to learn from other conflicts? The question was asked earlier on about resources, and I thought I'd save the plug until later one of the things we do is produce a journal called Accord, on peace processes. We've been doing it for 30 years and there are now 30 editions of it. And it's a comprehensive review of comparative experience of peacemaking. We get people who are involved in their processes to document and talk about their processes. It's all available online on our website. So delve into it – I think it's a fascinating compendium of how conflicts change.

Comparative learning is about generating, documenting evidence of what works, learning how to communicate and share it. But, and we do a lot of work that is about thought work, it's also about providing people opportunities to widen their horizons.

An example of this are the many study visits we have organised over the years, taking people from one context to another context.

The Northern Ireland experience has been a very powerful opportunity. And there are people in Northern Ireland who speak extraordinarily eloquently about the process of change they've been through.

One of the experiences I was most struck by was when we took some people to the Philippines to work with colleagues who were involved in the peace process in the Philippines, which was in some ways a couple or three years ahead of the n experience. And we took a couple of different groups. One was a group of women activists from Colombia, including the most senior woman police officials in Colombia, and including people from a diversity of communities. And actually the journey in itself was a peace process for them because they had to spend 10 days with one another from all spectrums, learning what was happening in the Philippines.

So structuring such study visits in a smart way can be an extraordinary learning opportunity. And it combined people into a community of how they then work together on return. And we've done many different sorts of things like that, learning about new ideas. We've been doing a lot of work in the last 18 months to 2 years, on what we call future thinking. How do you bring in fresh ideas and perspectives and help communities that are stuck in protracted conflicts? People often talk about intractable conflicts. I personally don't like the term intractable because I think our job as peacebuilders is to help people find traction and to find ways out, not to succumb to the language of "you can't do anything about this".

Bringing in new ideas, like futures thinking, is one part of this. We've been doing this with colleagues in the South Caucasus, in Kashmir and in Ethiopia. And it's fascinating to see how they seize on the reframing of their dilemmas, trying to project forward to what they would like to see their societies look like, and then working back to what are the component steps to get there.

In essence, a lot of what we do in that domain is what we call moving from practice to policy. How do you learn from what you're doing in context? How do you articulate that in a way that helps people in other contexts learn and deploy ideas? And how do you keep refreshing that process?

A second area of our work that I think is critical as peacebuilders is around bridging divides. The nature of violent conflict is it entrenches divides between communities, between people who may have at times lived together more or less comfortably - not just coexisted, but actually lived together constructively. And for different reasons, and every conflict has its own pathology, they become immersed in violent conflict and then it becomes, it seems almost impossible to bridge those divides.

And yet you will find people in the societies who strive to work with people across the conflict divide. And it can be incredibly difficult, it can be dangerous, it can be politically difficult, it can be difficult to resource it. And so often times they will need an outside actor to enable them to bridge those divides. And we do a lot of that. One example that for me has been fascinating and very personal has been work we've done in Kashmir over the last 20 years, bringing people across the line of control in Kashmir together to develop opportunities for trade across the line of control, to develop opportunities for educational initiatives, to do work on environmental and disaster management and to start trying to shape political discourse and to bring together people from within Kashmir, who are so neglected and ignored, into discourse with people in Delhi and Islamabad to try and shape ideas.

Now, you might quite rightly say, well, Kashmir doesn't seem to be any closer to a constructive outcome than it has for generations. And that's absolutely true. Yet what I find fascinating is there are people there who get ignored, who are doing courageous and constructive things to transform relationships. And it's all too easy to forget about that kind of incremental work that might put roots in place that mean that when the tectonic plates of the politics shift, change can happen. And so part of our role is how do you connect, how do you create linkages and how do you support those linkages to survive in the face of quite challenging circumstances?

Then I wanted to flag another type of connecting, what I'd call connecting the disconnected, work we've been doing in the Central African Republic, another context that is so far off the map that most people don't even think about, that there might be conflicts there. And yet for 15, 20 years, there's been some intense and challenging conflict there.

We've been working with communities in the periphery of the state who are often ignored by the political level negotiations at the centre, to connect them through what we call a decentralised dialogue into the centre of the political community. And one of the things that has been absolutely fascinating has been to see how in a society that has experienced extraordinary trauma over a generation, how they try and go about reconciliation using traditional approaches, but also trying to integrate more contemporary approaches to dealing with mental health and psychosocial trauma in a conflict situation. And that's a whole different discussion, but it's an example of different ways you need to connect and bridge divides.

The next area I wanted to just flag is about providing challenge. This is about building a relationship to put you in a position where you can work with people who have to ask themselves the hard questions and might not always be prepared to ask themselves the hard questions.

We work in the Somali regional state of Ethiopia, often called the Ogaden,, where there had been a civil war for 25 years. We were invited in to work by the Ogaden National Liberation Front, the ONLF, to support them when they received an invitation by the Ethiopian government to engage in peace talks back in 2012. A six year process led to the signing of a peace agreement. And since that peace agreement, in fact, the Ogaden has been the most stable part of Ethiopia and has been developing in a quite constructive way. One of the roles we were able to play here was to challenge thinking through research and analysis we were able to do in the context (which was not easy because it was a very closed environment) and with diaspora communities, and then to present findings to the leadership for them to reflect on their strategies. Another thing that I think is critical that outside actors can do is to provide solidarity. The people who are engaged within their own societies to transform those situations of violence can be very lonely. They're often exposed to great danger. And anyone who's worked in conflict contexts will sadly know people who've been killed as a result of their efforts to bring about peace. So to be an outside actor who they know cares about them and who they know brings ideas and resources can mean an awful lot to the morale of people facing often seemingly impossible situations.

Then another part of our role that I think is critical is trying to access resources, generate funds. Don't get me started on the ridiculousness of the expenditure on militarization compared to how much is put into peacebuilding. The peace process I mentioned in the Ogaden over six years, supporting a peace process that led to a peace agreement that brought to an end a 25 year conflict, cost us less than the price of half a tank. And I checked on eBay, tanks these days go for about 5 million pounds. So we spent less than 2 million pounds over a six year period that helped to bring to an end the 25 year conflict.

The problem is donors will all too often fund a one year project when everyone knows the peace process is a multi-year endeavour. So there's a real dissonance there. Part of our role is to try and generate the resources to support the people in context to keep doing their work. There's a lot more one could say on that, but in the interest of time, I won't go into it now.

So what makes this work? I think one of the things you have to ask yourself as an organisation doing this is what are your values, that inform why you do what you do? And how do you then build your mission and your strategy on the basis of those values? For Conciliation Resources, we frame our values around collaboration, creativity, commitment, and challenge. But at the heart of that, I think a critical dimension is understanding how relationships work, having the curiosity, the humility to explore relations, having the patience to work in situations that are protracted and seemingly impossible. And having the patience to not give up when it feels like you're not making progress.

It's also critical that you think about how you coordinate and create complementarity between the multiplicity of actors who are doing this work, because you're not doing it alone.

Sometimes you're treading on the toes of other organisations and sometimes you get into very uncomfortable situations. Peace-builders conflict with one another sometimes. So you really have to think about how you work with others. You have to ask yourself about your experience of success and failure and you will often fail in what you're trying to do. And you have to think what's your expectations of the change that you can bring about? And I think it's really important to recognize that change is often incremental.

I have colleagues who have dedicated 10, 20, 30 years to working in contexts where it might feel like you're not seeing progress and yet they have changed the lives of many people through that work in the relationships that they have with people who are doing the work in context. And so building those relationships and sustaining them is really critical to this kind of work.

I think it's also fundamentally important to realise that peacebuilding work - how can I put this? - often times donors will want to talk about the importance of people to people contacts. They'll say "Let's do that without getting involved in the politics" You can't do that. Conflict, violent conflict, is fundamentally about politics; peacebuilding is fundamentally about politics; and you have to navigate and understand that politics, if you're to make a contribution.

It's also about how do you manage the power asymmetries that exist in a society? Conflicts by their nature are often between parties that have different access to power. And one or other of those parties will feel that another party has more power and is using that power to oppress them.

So how do you navigate that? One of the things that often escapes attention is that you have to do an awful lot of work with communities separately before you try and bring them together. It's not just about thinking that some alchemy happens when you put people in a room together. If you haven't enabled them to develop how they'll act and how they'll change their relationships when they get into those situations, you do them a disservice. Trying to find the capacity to do that work in separate communities can be really tough, but I think it's critical.

So as I draw to a close, I want to try and end with a sort of hint of concern. Not a hint – now a shout of concern, but a hint of optimism. The concern is that the field of conflict resolution and peacebuilding conflict transformation is at risk of being squeezed by the increasingly militarised securitised approach to diplomacy that we see in the modern world. And I think that creates a real dilemma for us. We could have had a conversation here at great length about the double standards we see in the world of state led conflict resolution at the moment.

And this squeezes the space for people who are trying to approach the issues from a different perspective. So that gives me real concern when we think about what's happening in Europe, in Russia, in response to Russia's invasion of Ukraine and in the Middle East, in response to the generational conflict that persists and tragically experiences a constant metamorphosis into different levels of horror.

But I struggle because sometimes I feel pessimistic and I think, how do I hold onto my optimism in doing this work? And one of the things that enables me to remain optimistic is that I think there are more people having more intelligent conversations and engaged in thinking and practice around peacebuilding and supporting mediation than there have been in the past three decades of my engagement in this work.

We haven't got a critical mass, but we are having an impact. I see more and more governments having negotiations and mediation departments and often times you're working with people inside those foreign ministries who are working against the grain of their own ministry, but they're inside doing the thinking and talking to people outside and engaging in tremendously constructive ways.

I see a multiplicity of organisations engaged in this. I was for six years the chair of something called the European peace-building Liaison Office, EPLO, a network of European peace-building organisations. When I took on the role, there were 30 members, now there are 55 members and while it's hard to resource the work, there are more and more people doing this. And I think that's incredibly encouraging.

So I think we have to continue thinking how we prioritise a dialogical mediatory approach to conflict, as opposed to a militarised approach. We have to continue to pursue efforts that are both cognizant of the state but can go beyond, below, around the state. Because it is not about what states can do – it's about what societies can do, and how they can hold states to account for the purpose that states are there for - to attend to the needs of the people and populations within them. And I think we have to do a lot to redefine what we mean by success because these are generational conflicts we are dealing with, and you cannot think of short term gains in the face of the need for much longer-term outcomes. And ultimately to use a term that Diana has popularised there's an awful lot of transactional work in the world of humanitarian development and peacebuilding endeavour, therefore we have to make sure we hold onto the transformational dimension of what we do and not succumb to that transactional dimension. And it isn't easy.

And when you run an organisation and when you share responsibility for a group of 70 or people who are doing the work, you are of course concerned about the wellbeing and the opportunities for those colleagues to continue doing their work. But you've got to hold onto the fact of the transformational aspiration as to why you do this work and the people you're doing it with, who are living in contexts that are so much less able to live with the comfort that we live with here.

So thank you.

Diana: Brilliant. So let's have some questions and we'll give this 10 minutes please.

Questions to Jonathan Cohen

Q1: Jonathan, you talked about asking the hard questions and I see this, I see everywhere that people when they ... My activity is mostly around climate change and I see that people avoid saying the thing that the other person doesn't want to say. The people use circumlocutions and so on. And you, I thought about what you said about the group that you talked to and put the question to them - could you say some more about that? I think it's so important that we start to say clearly what it is we mean because, I mean otherwise, it doesn't happen.

A: Thank you. And of course it happens in many domains.

In that particular case, the Ogaden National Liberation Front had fought a War of Independence - they were striving for independence. And we had been looking at what people in the Somali Regional State wanted. The leadership was outside the region because they had had to flee for good reason, and they were a bit detached from what was happening in context. And it was very difficult to do work because it was essentially an authoritarian region, the way it was governed. But we managed to find ways of doing some research and getting a sense of what people in the communities wanted. And for them, independence wasn't a critical thing - they wanted a decent life.

And so the conversation we had to have with them was: are you in touch with what your community wants? And is it really independence? Self-determination is an incredibly powerful term in our field, but it doesn't always mean independence. It might mean you're prepared for some form of autonomy, but that's very difficult because it implies that you're giving up on your aspiration. So the conversation in that instance was around what does self-determination really mean and how do you work with the Ethiopian government to find a means to explore whether you can actually exist comfortably within a federal state of Ethiopia, with all the dysfunctions and problems that it has? Or do you really need to fight for independence and what's going to be the best for your people?

And a small addendum to that, several months after that meeting, a peace agreement had been signed and I was in Addis Ababa. One of the people who'd been most vocal in that meeting was deployed to Ethiopia to be the representative of the ONLF in Addis for the next phase of the discussions. And we met for lunch and he came running up to me waving his mobile phone at me and he showed me a picture of his four sisters. And he said "Last week, I saw my sisters for the first time in 25 years". And he said "That's what peace means". Brilliant.

Q2: I've got a question which is connected with the work I'm doing, which is researching the long term causes of the Falkland Islands War. And I wondered if you ever deal with internal things, actually parts of the United Kingdom, that have problems. Because, after all, that conflict caused a thousand deaths. Half the British Navy sank and still after 42 more years, there are no talks.

A: So, one of the questions we've been asking ourselves in recent times is, should we be looking at questions of conflict within the UK, and Marigold and I were talking at lunchtime about the racist violence that we saw recently – should organisations like ours be engaging in that in the UK? We don't, we don't feel we've got the expertise or the connections or the credibility to do that. But I think some of the lessons that we've been learning are applicable and there are conversations about how that can be deployed, but we haven't got to that point yet.

We don't work on the Falkland conflict as such. It's interesting because it feels like it's at the bottom of the compost heap almost at the moment. I mean, we do have to ask ourselves what sort of context can we work in, being the organisation we are? We don't work in situations of high intensity violence because we don't have the capacity to provide security to do that.

We work in situations of violent conflict, we work in places where we can have a long-term engagement where we think we can resource it, where we have an invitation to work with people in that society and where we feel we have the legitimacy and credibility to continue doing it.

One of the challenges in our field is to think about what does impartiality mean? Or some people talk about multi-partiality. At what point are you in a position where you can have the confidence of the parties to the conflict to continue playing a role? And there are people who very adeptly navigate being from within a community and working on their own conflict. And in fact, some of the most creative people we work with are what often in our field get called insider mediators, people who are from the context who are actually playing the dynamic roles.

So it doesn't exclude it, but we've chosen not to play that role in our own society to date. And maybe that'll change – I know I've got some colleagues who are agitated to do more of that.

Q3: Thanks Jonathan, I thought that was so interesting. For lots of people who won't have any contact with peacebuilding work themselves or with accompanying people in situations of violent conflict, what would you say people can do from the UK to support that sort of approach, whether it's asking for certain kinds of policies from the UK government or some other kind of …… ?

A: So, I think first of all, be better informed. I think we'll all be aware that an awful lot of conversations happen about an awful lot of conflicts where people bandy around opinions that are ill-informed and it can feed into antagonism. So being better informed is really important. Support organisations that are doing peace-building work, read our documents, learn from that, and there is a community of us: Conciliation Resources, Peace Direct, Saferworld, International Alert, Concordis – a range of organisations in the UK. We'll hear Gwen talk about an organisation. I mean there are a multitude of organisations out there in the world doing incredible work.

But I think there is something that can be done, which is thinking about how to talk to the political community in this country, and it's something we've not been as good at as we need to get. We need to be better, and it's something we are developing. And thinking about how messages are conveyed, what expectations are made.

Final very quick point. We did a survey six or seven years ago, a public opinion survey about people's appetite for engaging with armed groups. Now, there used to be a discussion 20 years ago, can you talk to terrorists? So we talk about engaging with armed groups and we did a survey because we wanted to show to the government, our assumption was that people actually are more open to that than the politicians seem to be prepared to be. And we did surveys here in the UK and four other countries and it showed that there's an appetite to engage with people if you think it's leading towards a constructive outcome.

And there's a constant case to be made to convince politicians to put more money into peacebuilding - and we heard some good comments about that earlier – but not just to put money into organisations like us, because we're a tiny, tiny drop in the ocean. To transform the way their politics works. And to transform the way the politicians perceive engagement in violent conflict and the transformation of that into different types of societies.

And I think Paul and John and Diana spoke eloquently about that.

So thank you and just to say, I've got a couple of publications, so catch me afterwards. I'll be happy to share things with you.

Colin: Accord is a fantastic publication. You really have to see it. I've got many of the back copies. It's one of the best things I've seen around talk to terrorists. Well actually people were always talking to terrorists. And of course it's better not to label them terrorists because it builds those very relationships, you can sometimes help people reframe and revise what they're trying to do to reach their political objectives. Again, it's a long story and all these contexts are long stories.

Colombia Case Study

GWEN BURNYEAT

Dr Gwen Burnyeat is an Assistant Professor in Social Anthropology at the University of Edinburgh, currently researching the role of stories in polarisation and bridge-building in Colombia and Britain. She is a political anthropologist, writer, and peace-builder, with over 14 years' experience working on peace and politics in Colombia as both scholar, practitioner, and producer of award-winning ethnographic documentary Chocolate of Peace. She is an active member of peace-building organisation Rodeemos el Diálogo (ReD, or "Embrace Dialogue").

It's really wonderful to be here and thank you so much, the Movement for the Abolition of War, for the invitation. I just want to say I'm really inspired by the whole day, all of the speakers and also the work that you guys are doing as an organisation, because I really believe in civil society support for peace, and what that can do.

I'm going to talk a bit about civil society peacebuilding in the Colombian case, using the example of an organisation I belong to called "Rodeemos el Diálogo" or Embrace Dialogue. I want to apologise for the absence of my husband who was also on the list, in the invitation earlier, who was one of the co-founders of Embrace Dialogue. He would have loved to be here, but he's involved in a peace negotiation in Colombia at the moment with a small splinter group of a guerilla group in Colombia. So he thought that was a good excuse and he's there doing the work. I'll be talking about the work that we've been doing together in Embrace Dialogue in Colombia, but to get to that point, I want to tell you a bit about how I got to be doing this.

I'm a political anthropologist, I'm a lecturer at the University of Edinburgh, but I'm wearing a couple of different hats because I'm also part of Embrace Dialogue and I first went to work in Colombia, not as an anthropologist, but part of an organisation which many of you may be familiar with called Peace Brigades International. I did peace building accompaniment work, in a war zone in Colombia, in the Northwest, and this turned my life upside down in the best possible way, because I was working with communities who were resisting forced displacement in the midst of the war, and one of them in particular I was very captivated by, called the Peace Community of San Jose, who are a peasant farmer community who are trapped between left wing guerillas, right wing paramilitaries and state armed forces, and decided to declare themselves neutral to the armed conflict as a way of staying on their land and resisting involvement from all sides.

I ended up then retraining as an anthropologist. My background was in literature, so I went to the National University of Colombia in Bogotá and I spent two years studying anthropology there and going back and forth between Bogotá and the peace community in this region I've been working with, to write a thesis, which then became my first book.

I'm telling you this because I think that the peace community is a good example of one form of peace building, which I think many of us would believe very much in, a community grassroots bottom-up approach to peace building, very much based in practices of land cultivation. They produce organic fair trade cacao, which they sell to Lush cosmetics, (the smelly soap shop.) My book is actually called Chocolate, Politics and Peace Building and there's a film called Chocolate of Peace, which you can look up. It's a very bottom-up grassroots philosophy of peace building involving relationship to land, historical memory about the mass atrocities they've suffered, solidarity economics and things like that. But it's also a good case that illustrates the impact of the Colombian civil war on the civilian population.

A couple of brief words on Colombia, for those who aren't familiar with the case. In many ways, Colombia's been going through 200 years of war, each kind of war after independence recycled into the next. But the latest is what's generally called the internal armed conflict.

It started in the 1960s between left-wing guerilla groups that emerged to overthrow the state, which they have not been able to do in all of this time. And then the state was fighting back and then also created paramilitary groups, which got out of hand and have become, also, very, very powerful in their own right; right wing paramilitary groups.

And all of this, of course, is very much contaminated by drug trafficking. Everyone is involved in trafficking and that has degraded the political conflict component of the war. It's still a political war, but this has been going on for now 60 years, with all of these different groups, and those most affected have been the civilian population. There's been over, I think in the latest numbers, over 10 million victims of conflict, different patterns of violations from multiple forced displacement. So, we're talking over seven or 8 million forced displacements, many of them internally displaced. I think it's the highest number of forced displacements after Syria. Jonathan might have more up to date figures on that; massacres, torture, landmines, sexual violence in the context of war, forced disappearances, well over double that of the whole of the southern cone. It's a massive, massive impact on the civilian population. And communities in rural areas like the one I was working with have borne the brunt of it. They have suffered all of those patterns of violations, mass forced displacement, massacres, torture, et cetera, et cetera.

I was working with them, living in Bogotá when Embrace Dialogue started in 2012, in London, actually, between Colombians and friends of Colombia, people like me who'd been living in Colombia, who'd been involved in peacemaking initiatives in Colombia in various ways.

They got together because peace talks began between the government and the biggest guerilla group, the FARC, this was in 2012, and they felt they wanted to literally surround the dialogue. In Spanish Rodeemos means to surround. So, they wanted to rally around the dialogues, the peace dialogues, and find ways of contributing to them to help them achieve a successful peace agreement from civil society. Then Andrei and myself started the Colombian chapter of Rodeemos el Dialogo in 2014 and so there I was living in Bogotá, having had my inauguration into Colombia in this very different, war zone. And for me, that was Colombia.

I'd fallen in love with Colombia in this rural peace building context, with colleagues and friends and people who I had admired and learned from, who were really experiencing the everyday consequences of war: helicopters flying overhead and being terrified that they might drop a bomb, not being able to go off a particular track where you're farming because there might be a landmine there. And they were really, really living with death threats all the time. And then suddenly we were in Bogotá and nobody knew what was going on. Nobody knew what was happening in their own country! And I, as a foreigner, I felt this was very strange, I couldn't really understand it. And we started off having these little spaces of dialogue in a little restaurant in Bogotá called Peace Breakfasts. Every Saturday we would get together with a group of some 20 people, initially friends, then friends of friends.

Then we set up a mailing list and then friends of friends of friends. And then we started to advertise it on social media and people started to come. And initially they were just spaces to talk about the peace process that was beginning with the FARC to try to work out what we knew, share information, become more aware. And then we began to develop a methodology that grew. We would invite a speaker each time who would be someone with some kind of expertise, either a government negotiator or an academic, or a former combatant or a victim of the conflict who could come and sit down with 25 people from Bogotá and explain their take on peace, the peace process with the FARC and peace building. The people who came were very varied. Some of them knew a lot about peace. Some of them were academics or peace policymakers, involved in the policy world. Some of them had nothing to do with peace at all, or politics, and they didn't know anything, but they felt that this was an important thing that was happening in their country and they wanted to be informed and they wanted to be involved in some way.

And so the format was not about giving a talk. There was a 20 minute bit where the speaker would engage in a kind of semi-structured conversation with a facilitator, and then we would open it out over breakfast, which included hot chocolate produced by the peace community that I had brought back, because peace begins with food, and sharing food with people is a really good way of building intimacy, and people began to talk and share their own views and ask questions. And we began to see that actually dialogue itself was just as important as supporting the big macro political dialogues that were happening in Cuba.

And so I was there learning about why people in Bogotá didn't really know or seem to care what was happening in the conflict region I'd been working in. And initially I was kind of angry about that, and then I began to think, well, actually as a white European, what right have I got to be angry about what people in Bogotá know and don't know? And I began to understand also that they'd lived a completely different experience of the war. And I think this is something that I was very struck by. In every country there's a divorce between the countryside and the city. I'm from London, I have no idea what the life of a rural sheep farmer is like in Wales, there's a gap between our experiences. We haven't met each other, I don't know what their everyday life is like. In a country where war has taken place primarily in the countryside, that gap is magnified a thousand fold. And that's what I think had happened. I began to understand that people in Bogotá hadn't had the opportunity to meet people like the Peace Community.

They'd never had the privilege that an international peace builder has of being able to go to a conflict region relatively safely and meet these incredibly articulate and inspiring people. So then I brought people from the Peace Community to Bogotá to be the special guests at the Peace Breakfast. And I saw how transformative that was when you could bring people together. This was not about who was on whose side in the war.

What I want to talk about from this case study today is a bit about the wider society's perception of war and peace, and peace efforts.

We discovered how much people needed to talk, not just about the different experiences of war that had happened, but also about politics and about the country and about the 'abouts' that the war was ostensibly about, about land or about victims' reparations or about political participation, about indigenous rights, and so since then, 2014 when we started, (that's a picture from 2015), we've now had more than 300 peace breakfasts in Colombia, as well as some 250 other kinds of dialogue events, from salons to conversation evenings to academic round tables and conferences about different aspects of peace, politics and reconciliation.

A lot of peacebuilding initiatives often focus on reconciliation as a process that happens between, say, victims and perpetrators, or between enemy combatants. And there's been a lot of very important stuff like that in Colombia, of people who've brought together former guerilla fighters with former soldiers, for example. And they find out they've got more in common than they actually thought. People who've remembered shooting at each other across battlefields, being able to meet each other and think, gosh, how lucky we were not to have killed each other in that moment! And also between victims and people who've caused them harm. And of course, as Diana said, people do sometimes forgive.

Not everyone can, but people do, and when they do, it's incredibly inspiring to listen to; but you can do a lot of that work and still not have broader citizen support for peace, which we started to think about as involving the "disorganised" civil society, not the victims organisations, not the really educated, incredibly inspiring social movements there are in Colombia of all sorts, women's organisations, indigenous organisations, LGBT, academics, students, I mean incredible civil society organisations, but actually the people who aren't involved in those are also really important.

We discovered how important it was in 2016 when there was a peace deal reached between the government and the FARC guerillas. It was celebrated globally by peace experts as one of the most comprehensive peace accords to date in the world, because not only did it promise to disarm the FARC, it also was looking at making structural reforms to prevent future spirals of violence for land reform, political participation, tackling the drug trafficking, which has fuelled the war, providing redress and reparations to the victims of the conflict. And yet the government decided to hold a referendum on the peace deal. This was three months after Brexit. I was here for Brexit, and then I was back in Colombia for October 2016. And the Colombian public voted no by 50.2% to the peace deal, and it really created a massive 'before and after' in Colombian politics and history.

There are many reasons for the loss of the referendum which I won't go into. We can talk about it if you're interested afterwards, my second book was partly about this. One of them has to do with the opposition to the peace accord led by the right wing, a right wing party who led a 'no' campaign, which made the Brexit bus look like a gospel of truth!

Also because of a lot of very difficult feelings around the peace accord because for many people, it wasn't necessarily only about the politics, it was also about what does it mean to see the guerilla go into politics? What does it mean to see the guerilla not go to jail? How do you cope with those emotions after 50 years of war? So much suffering, which has touched so many people in so many different ways.

So the referendum was a disaster. And although the deal was renegotiated and is being implemented, it suffers from a major legitimacy deficit, which resulted from that vote and a polarisation of the country, which has continued and evolved and attached itself to different political processes ever since. And in some ways, I think this is interesting because somehow polarisation is actually a sign of peace: you are having the conflict through politics rather than through weapons, so in some ways that's a good thing, but it also in some context has concrete implications on people's lives because this legitimacy deficit blocked implementation of the peace deal. And it meant that all of the efforts to implement the peace deal got stuck in Congress or got watered down. This was compounded by the fact that one of the leaders of the 'no' campaign then won the presidency a year and a half later, and, although he couldn't renege on the deal, because it had been signed, it was a state policy, he didn't want to implement it fully or he was criticised for implementing it very partially.

And so this question of political will, which we've been hearing about all morning, is really a massive cornerstone of peace accords, and it also created a climate of justification of violence. Since the signing of the accord, something like, I can't remember the numbers, about a thousand activists of various kinds have been assassinated. Over 300 members of the

FARC who laid down their weapons in good faith to transition into politics have also been killed. Some of them feeling that there were no security guarantees for them to do politics have gone back to war and taken up arms again. There's been a fragmentation of different armed groups who have filled the gaps of power left by the FARC when they disarmed, because the parts of the agreement, which were to do with filling those power gaps and building state presence in those areas, were not really implemented.

So there's been a lot of violent conflict which has resulted from the referendum in some ways indirectly as well.

After this Rodeemos el Dialogo has redoubled its efforts to try to reach different sectors of society and build a wider climate for peace and build what we call a culture of dialogue. We've gone from thinking about surrounding the national dialogues to building a culture of dialogue, as to what it means to build peace from civil society. And so we've done a number of different, other sorts of efforts. We do something called Peace Pedagogy, which involves, I'd like to say they're workshops, we call them 'non workshops' because we think people are sick of workshops. So we do 'non workshops', in which we go into different educational institutions, schools, companies and businesses and all sorts of different institutions to do non workshops about the peace process to help people engage with their emotions about the peace process, but also develop new awareness and understanding about what was going on and what continues to be going on. Also about reconciliation and also about the Truth Commission, which is one of the institutions that was set up by the Peace Accord in 2016.

This is a picture of a more recent peace pedagogy initiative of talking to people about the contents of the Truth Commission, which listened to victims and perpetrators and documented the past. Of course, talking about the past is a very important part of peace building. We also do work here in the UK as I mentioned to you, this began among Colombians living in the UK, and Andrei and I have gone back and forth from Colombia at different moments. There's also groups of different people doing work here with diaspora communities, with academia and with government and policy world. And it's mostly volunteer run. We've got people doing research following the developments in Colombia, communications, and one of the most rewarding things has been to see the transformation in members who join, young people who spend a few years with Rodeemos el Dialogo and then take the philosophy forward into their own lives, and see their commitment to dialogue as a way of coexisting with difference in disagreement.

I want to finish by talking, putting my academics hat on because Rodeemos el Dialogo has inspired me to undertake a new research project about bridge building, and I think bridge building is different from peace building, but it can be a really important part of it. Bridge building is an iterative process of building cross-cutting relationships across different sets of society who are not necessarily involved in conflict, but who are witnessing what's going on and thinking about it, to develop wider understanding and empathy for difference, and humanising the myriad others that we live among.

And finding spaces to coexist with different forms of otherness.

And I like the concept of 'xenopolis', which is proposed by a Polish theorist, and practitioner called Krzystof Czyżewski ("jujevsky"), and he describes xenopolis as an aspirational coexistence, which doesn't seek to minimise difference and emphasise what we have in common, which is sometimes the problem with these liberal kind of narratives that we have, but actually imagines a kind of world constituted of others, and embracing otherness, the condition of political community with all the discomforts and identity conflicts that this entails.

This kind of bridge building, it's not necessarily about mediation or conflict transformation that Diana was talking to us about, it's about finding a greater understanding of living together. I think this is important for building a wider social fabric for peace. As Jonathan mentioned, you need the top down, you need state interventions, you can't do it without top down politics, but there are windows of opportunity which can open and windows of top-down politics align and open, and you need the social fabric and the citizen support for peace there to rise up and respond, because citizen support for peace processes is crucial to prevent derailing or rejection like with the referendum. Peace is political in all senses of the word, and I think that that's important not only for countries at war like Colombia, but also places like the UK where we're experiencing an increased concern about other forms of conflict and violence. Basically we need dialogue and bridge building to get better at living with political friction.

Thank you.

Diana: That's brilliant. It is amazing, because this is really different and also terrific and also so important, and you've ended up at a point just where somebody in the audience was talking this morning about the need to deal with the big conflicts growing in our own country. So it's really fantastic. Thank you.

Questions to Gwen Burnyeat

Q.(Rebecca Johnson): Thank you very much. That was very interesting for me to hear it from that perspective. I guess I've been involved to a small extent back and forth as a part of the Women In Black network with Ruta Pacifica, which is a women's organisation that goes back and forth between the centre of Bogotá and doesn't have that with the rural areas, for many, many, many years, I've only known them for 15 now.

You spoke about the power differential and quite a number of people have here, but there's also an experiential or experience differential in which the experience of women at all the levels, but often working at the grassroots level, because women often go into those areas of the most marginalised and most silenced of the communities, where armed violence has the most impact, which is on women and girls in many, many, many conflicts.

And yet really it's hardly been mentioned, so far today, that recognition that those with power, there may be a differential between the civil society and the governmental, those with power, but actually those with power still benefit massively more from being able make a career out of being, being able to do this kind of work.

And reconciliation in that context is actually an issue of power because of who gets to choose at what point or at what level reconciliation takes place.

I've just spent two weekends of constant meetings of Women In Black online conference where we were hearing from the silenced women of Afghanistan. We heard from Ruta Pacifica, not silenced, but very strong, but with a very different perspective perhaps. We were hearing from the silenced women trying to get projects going in DR Congo, facing extractivism for minerals that are supposed to save our climate. I haven't been hearing those perspectives even mentioned today, and I'd like you to maybe reflect that back to me with just a few words.

A. Yeah, Ruta Pacifica is one of the most important.

It's a platform organisation in Colombia of women that groups together lots of different localised women's organisations, and they've been going for decades and they're one of these amazingly impressive civil society organisations I mentioned, and they do, as you say, move between Bogotá and centres of power, and they have a recognition that enables them to talk to government and talk to international community, but also, working with local women in different places.

I really like what you said about reconciliation being an issue of power.

I don't think you asked a question, I think you just said something very valid and I wanted to add something to it, which is that women's organisations have been so influential in Colombia. They've done really amazing things. They were able to organise nationally, during the peace negotiations, and complain to the government and the FARC, why haven't you got any women negotiators in your teams? And as a result, they put women negotiators in their teams, both of them.

And then there was a women's, gender sub that was created to ensure a transversal gender focus in the peace accord, which is the first time that's ever happened in a global peace process.

So women have been able to achieve really amazing things, but I think that this experiential differential, the differential between different experiences of war is so important when thinking about reconciliation because those women's organisations that have such power that international peace builders look up to, they are very unknown among the female feminist business elites in Colombia, for example.

So that, when I say like, we need to look at broader society, I think that's really important.

And there's a really impressive woman who we've done some work with called Bertha Friera, who's a very elite business woman who was a victim of one of the FARC bombs in a social club in Bogotá.

And what she does now is she organises dialogues, and one of the dialogues she's been doing recently is between former FARC combatant women, - one of the guerilla groups in the world with most female presence or participation, who are mostly of rural origin, who've lived the war, who've been fighting for a revolution, - with elite business women, which she's been able to do because she is an elite business woman. And she's brought them together to talk to each other, to hear about their different experiences. These local FARC women have demonised the capitalist elite all through the revolution.

And to sit down with them and hear what their experiences have been of kidnapping, what their experiences have been, of being afraid to go to work in certain regions, and then for those business women, who are some of the most high powered people in the country, to listen to what it's like to be a female combatant and to what it was like: they've stigmatised the guerillas for years, for being terrorists, for being drug traffickers, for raping women, and to hear their real experiences.. I think these processes of dialogue among women can be incredibly powerful.

Thank you.

Diana: Thank you. Thank you. Brilliant. Really brilliant. And that end of it - also a brilliant addition.

Myanmar Case Study

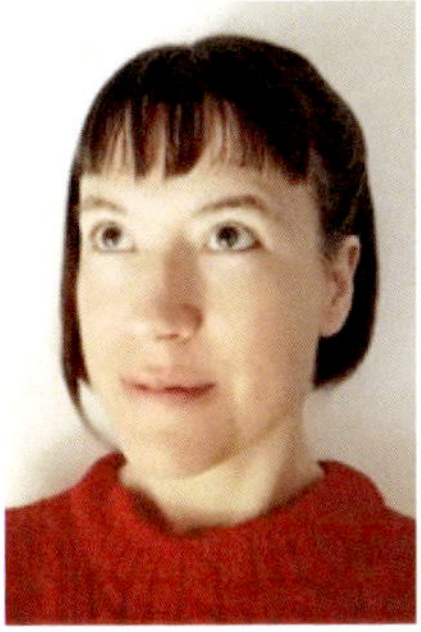

TANYA HUBBARD

Tanya Hubbard is a facilitator and trainer in conflict transformation and dialogue. Her passion is for using non-violent communication and creative approaches to enable people to re-connect compassionately with themselves, to re-humanise and connect with people who are 'other' and to collectively re-imagine a future of justice and peace. Some of her favourite tools for this are physical theatre, art with natural or recycled materials and storytelling.

Greetings everyone. My name is Tanya Hubbard. I'm sorry that I can't be with you in person in London today, but greetings to everyone who is there and everyone else who's online.

My presentation is going to focus on using physical theatre, playfulness and empathy as tools for community level dialogue. I'm going to share with you my work and my experience of doing that between 2013 and 2022 in areas of conflict in Myanmar. Just to start, I'd like to say that I understand this work as web weaving. I understand this work as strengthening the existing connections between people, between groups, between people who have different identities, strengthening what's already there and perhaps weaving new webs of connection. I also want to say that all of the images that I use throughout this presentation are either images that have been created by people in the workshops and spaces of dialogue that I've held in Myanmar or are photos of those spaces. I've deliberately blurred any photos of people in this presentation because being involved in anything related to peace and dialogue is currently very dangerous in Myanmar.

The approaches I'm going to talk about are inspired by and draw from very established approaches for holding spaces of dialogue at community level. We drew from Augusto Boal's work of the theatre of the oppressed. I drew heavily from training that I participated in that was led by Leap Confronting Conflict in London that merges Boal's work with CBT and with non-violent communication. We also drew heavily on a book that [John Paul] Lederach, wrote called When Blood and Bones Cry Out, which was very much for me about noticing the local cultural resources and rituals for peace that are already there and mobilizing those and leaning on those. This image here is of a traditional doll that is used all over Myanmar for children to play with. It's made from something like papier mache and it has usually a hard clay part at the bottom. You knock it over, you can smack it, you can really hurl it across the room and it always comes back up and rights itself again. This was a doll that we used often to explore resilience in difficult circumstances.

Throughout the work that I did and I was blessed to do this work in collaboration with local people who had different identities. So Burmese people of different identities and ethnic identities from different parts of Myanmar who had different skills, experiences, perspectives of what was happening and also with other international peace builders from Colombia particularly. And so we were constantly asking ourselves this tool, this perspective comes from somewhere else.

Does it work here?

Is it useful?

Is it doing harm?

What are the local practices that we can involve in this space?

And so we often involved a lot of local singing, dancing, games which had a huge impact on the energy in the space and the connection the connections created between people. So I'll speak about how we used the theatre of the oppressed to create spaces of dialogue and to create opportunities for dehumanization and for healing in areas of Myanmar. And theatre of the oppressed is a process that maybe some of you are familiar with. I'll give you a very, very whistle-stop tour of what it means. It means working with a group of let's say twenty people, twenty community members and taking them through a playful, physical, embodied process to explore local issues, challenges, conflicts. And then through a process of improvisation, again a very, very playful, laugh-based process - you can see in this picture that people are laughing. And this picture is actually taken in Rakhine, an area that the Rohingya fled from. And the interaction that we can see in this photo is a process that was that we were leading between the Rohingya people in this part of northern Rakhine and the local ethnic Rakhine people - most of them are Buddhist. And those two groups of people were in great conflict. There was simmering tension. There had been explosions of violence between the two peoples over various issues repeatedly over several years.

So it was a very tense situation. It was very delicate. But you can see from the faces of the people in this photo that this process of exploration enables something else to happen in the space. So through this process of exploration of local issues and improvisation together they gradually put together a theatre piece, a small sketch. It doesn't have to be perfect. It doesn't have to be, you know, something that is professional level. But it has an authenticity and it's grounded in local reality and local metaphors and local language in a way that makes it very, very real. And so they make this piece of theatre and they usually show the problem up into a particular moment. And then what happens is when we show the theatre to the community we invite them to participate. They go from being passive to being part of the conversation. And the piece of theatre is stopped and we say,

Do you have ideas?
What could be different here?
How could we change these challenges?
How could we change these power dynamics?
How could we create more connection here?
How could we create more empathy?

And either the people in the audience come in to the play and physically take on the role of someone in the piece or they can give suggestions that then the performers try out. So it's a way of playing with and exploring solutions in relation to real community problems. And this is really powerful because it enables a kind of shift from a sense of stuckness and despair which was very strong in this part of Myanmar, a sense of not being able to change very strong patterns of disconnection, hate and a very deep sense of disempowerment.

So this process of playing with exploring, trying ways of changing things can feel really, really empowering. And we did it in different parts of Myanmar. This process, we did it in a Rakheim state, Kachin state, Shan and we also worked with organisations who were working across the whole of Myanmar. We did this process with international NGOs often and also local NGOs, staff, volunteers and we also held the process independently with community members. So we're working with a real range of people in different parts of Myanmar. But when we were working, we were working mostly with people in living in camps for displaced people.

For example, we held this process to explore, as I just described to you, the intergroup tensions that were simmering in very dangerously in Rakheim. We also held this process with men and women in various different parts of Myanmar because there is a huge problem with domestic violence and violence against women and girls in communities that have been displaced and in communities that haven't been displaced. And so we held these spaces as opportunities for dialogue between men and women to explore the impact of that on everyone and to develop more empathy between men, women and children.

Another example is we held these processes for children and teenagers and adults to explore the impact of physical violence on children within the communities of displaced people. And I remember very vividly a moment when one of the camp leaders actually stepped in from being an audience member to being a member of the performers to take on the role of a child in the piece that was being played. And to try something to shift the power dynamics, to shift what was happening in that situation, it was amazing to see the child's face, realizing that the camp leader was going to step in and try and live his life and step into his shoes and also to see the reaction from the whole of the rest of the group to the way that these explorations and shiftings of power were enabling different kinds of conversations. We also held this process with women's groups in different parts of Myanmar in to explore how they participated in decision making and how they could influence camp leaders more to take into account the needs of women and girls.

And these processes, as I've said, were really powerful for various different reasons. Physical play takes people out of their normal modes of being. There's something that happens when we kind of stand up from sitting in a serious way with our bodies in a very kind of formal, often closed way and start to play together, start to move together, the physical theatre games that are involved in this process are often very silly, very playful, very joyful. They produce a lot of laughter, a lot of surprise from people. And so it takes people out of their normal mode of being and invites them into a different kind of explorative creative space where other things can happen. And that means also that divisions, because of identity, or because of something else, have the opportunity to be put aside as people go into this explorative way of being and connectedness can happen. And that's very clear physically when I hold these processes because people often come in and they're kind of nervous and tight and their bodies are closed, their shoulders are closed. You can see their jaws are tight. They're often they've got their arms crossed across their bodies, their legs across. And then as they play, there's something that happens here, there's an openness that happens. And there's a kind of fluidity in the body. And also you start to see people touching each other, holding hands, putting hands around each other, walking with hands held. So there are levels of physical connection that also become very clear as this process unfolds.

Another part of this that is really important is that it's accessible to anyone. Lots of the people that we work with in Myanmar had been denied access to education because they were displaced and also because of a very strategic approach by the central Darnies government to deny various different ethnic groups with access to education as part of a program of structural violence. And so lots of these people live with deep shame that they weren't literate, and that they had no access to lots of the information that was being shared in writing and lots of the ways of getting involved in making decisions or having an impact that involved writing. And so this process was amazing because it could be the poorest member of the community who had had absolutely no access to any education whatsoever who could come with the most amazing creative idea about changing a community or finding a solution for a community challenge. It was often the people who we wouldn't expect who came with this capacity for creativity and this capacity for also empathy for other people.

The other thing about this approach is that it enables dialogue about really difficult topics. If you're just sitting in a room in a circle or if you're sitting in a room with kind of tables and chairs lined up, that can be a fear that means that some topics just can't be touched because they're too taboo, they're too hot for a conversation to happen. But once you start moving and sharing and playing and creating connection in this way, then dialogue can happen even on really difficult topics.

So domestic violence is a very taboo topic but in this picture you can see my colleague, she is using a pen to pretend to hold a microphone to someone's voice to interview a member of the performing team to explore what that character is feeling, what's happening, what she needs, what her challenges are. And the same in relation to inter-group conflicts, this process enabled those things to be named with tenderness but with clarity because when we're showing it also physically in sculptures or in pieces of theatre, then there's a clarity in that because we're showing it with our bodies. So there are some things we don't have to say because they've already been shown physically.

The other important thing about this is that in a situation where people have been displaced and have felt enormously disempowered because they might have lost their land, lost their jobs, lost their roles, lost their sense of self, lost a sense of dignity. And in this situation often decisions are made by people who come from outside, whether that's people who come from other countries and bring their ideas and their cultures and their solutions, or even just people from big cities who happen to have had more education and have roles of control in INGO or local NGOs or civil society. And so these processes are really different from that because the ideas and the solutions about what to do differently come from the community members themselves. This process of playing is about them finding the solution and them exploring together whether something works or not. We can try something, it doesn't work, it doesn't matter, it's a safe space for exploration. They let it go, they try something else.

So this is really powerful in the sense of being a bottom-up process of both dialogue but also solution finding. And there's a psychosocial element to this process that I've already touched on. Bodies that are tight with fear and grief and hate because of very real threats around them of collective violence or violence from the military. They come loose in collective play. Shared laughter weaves bonds of connection between people who are of different ages, different genders, different identities, different religions. And there's a precious liminal moment of escape from all of the normal challenges, fears, worries that are so heavy on people living in displaced communities. They get to escape, they get to play, they get to be children, they get to laugh and that's very powerful.

The other part of this process is that we invite community members to share their stories, to share personal stories with each other. In this photograph you can see women in Shan State sharing their stories with each other. We ask them to share stories about things that are challenging, about issues that are troubling them.

And you can see from this picture about what that does, that creates empathy, that gives people the opportunity to understand and re-humanize people who might be different in some way. You might seem other but through this process of storytelling they discover that they're really not other, they're very similar. They share many of the same hopes, dreams, fears, challenges. And that process also enables a feeling of safety and trust to develop between people participating in this process.

We use non-violent communication constantly throughout these processes, so we're constantly exploring feelings, constantly exploring needs, constantly unpacking judgments, constantly checking for how to request things in a way that is actually compassionate and with empathy and results in a win-win situation for the people involved. That process has the impact of developing the capacity of people who take part in these processes to be aware of their own feelings and needs. And those are their family members and people close to them. That's often one of the biggest pieces of feedback to be get from these processes is that at the end, I have a self-awareness for myself, and for people around me that has really transformed my relationships. And it's an amazing tool for resilience in a really, really extraordinarily challenging situation. And as I've said, this process of testing, of playing, of trying enables community members to find new strategies for existing challenges, and to leave the process feeling more confident that they can actually handle and that they are creative and that they have value in their community and that they have more connection with each other. As I said at the beginning with that web metaphor, they have a sense of connection with other people, they have empathy and less fear.

I'm coming to the end of my presentation now but I can't finish without mentioning the current situation in Myanmar, because my work has for the moment needed to pause because the current civil war there is extremely difficult at the moment for people all over Myanmar. So I encourage you to remember Myanmar to think about the conflict that's happening there and to think about supporting it if you can. And I thank you for listening to my presentation and I wish you a good rest of the conference.

Thank you. Bye bye.

Philippines Case Study

Jonathan Cohen

I'm going to be talking about Conciliation Resources' work in the Philippines.

I'm going to talk about the mechanics of a peace process and how you can get to a peace agreement. And I'll do so through one particular case study in regard to Mindanao, the Bangsamoro region in the south of the Philippines.

We've seen on screen and Gwen shared some figures, a sort of shocking representation of the consequences of violent conflict.

So just to add to what we heard about and Myanmar, let me provide some background. This is a conflict that started in the late 1960s. The peace agreement, the comprehensive peace agreement was signed in 2014, and in the intervening period there were about 120,000 fatalities and 3 million people displaced. That gives you a sense of the scale of the violent conflict that we are talking about.

We are talking about the island of Mindanao, which is in the south of the Philippines. It has a strong Muslim community, called the Bangsamoro people, in a predominantly Christian country. There is definite religious dimension to this. But as with all conflicts, there are multiple dimensions to it: a self-determination claim; land ownership; we've heard a lot about identity; there's an indigenous community that often got ignored in the conflict.

The peace process had a number of phases. The violent phase started in the late sixties. In the early nineties you had the beginnings of a peace process. It led to the signing of an agreement in 1996 between the government and the Moro National Liberation Front (MNLF). And the war had essentially been one in which the people on the island of Mindanao were at war, not all of them, but the Moro people were striving for independence.

But in 1996, the Moro National Liberation Front signed an agreement about autonomy and the nature of political arrangements with a degree of self-determination. This led to a split between the MNLF, which was satisfied with autonomy, and the Moro Islamic Liberation Front (MILF), which was not.

The next phase of the conflict began with the MILF aspiring for independence. And from 1997 to 2000, you had what can be called the domestic phase of the peace process with the new government, a new government in the Philippines, trying to negotiate a deal with the MILF but not moving forward. From 2000 to 2008, you had what's often seen as the diplomatic phase of the negotiations. The government of the Philippines invited Malaysia to play a role as a facilitator. And you had diplomatic talks going on that didn't lead to a constructive outcome, and you had periods of resumed violence.

And then in 2008, after a particularly bad phase of escalation in the conflict, a reframing of what to do came about partly as a result of a new president being elected, President Aquino, the son of Cory Aquino, who had been a very dynamic actor and president previously. And the talks between the MILF and the government at that time led to the creation of a very unusual mechanism to support the peace process.

This is what I want to talk about, because you will have probably heard often times about groups of friends or troikas or quartets, when people on the news talk about peace processes, those are usually groups of states that help a mediator in their efforts.

In this instance, what's called a hybrid group was established, called the International Contact Group.

It comprised four states: Japan, because Japan had been doing a lot of development and infrastructure work in the Philippines; Saudi Arabia, because of its connection to the Organization of Islamic States, and its Muslim identity; Turkey also because of its Muslim identity, but also its long tradition of development work in Asia; and the United Kingdom, which was playing on its Northern Ireland experience. There was also a desire not to include Australia and the United States, in part because they were two regional big players.

The creative thing here was there was a recognition that for the MILF, states were a club that didn't want them as a member. So, the MILF pushed for, and it was agreed, that some non-state actors would be part of the contact group. Four NGOs were invited to join: an Indonesian social movement called Muhammadiyah; the Centre for Humanitarian Dialogue, which is one of the biggest and most experienced mediation support NGOs; the Asia Foundation, which is a substantial US-originated foundation working on social and political development throughout Asia; and Conciliation Resources - were invited to join by local civil society. As a result you had four NGOs and four states, and our role was to support the Malaysian facilitator.

Now it's interesting, the Malaysian role wasn't called a mediator, and this was intentional on the part of the parties. They didn't want a mediator who would assume more authority and mediate between them. They wanted a facilitator who'd play a back seat role, who'd be at their service to support their needs. It was all about giving agency and ownership to the conflict parties, which so often doesn't happen, and letting them navigate the direction.

The fact of having this unusual construction was really important. It meant that the asymmetrically weaker party, the Moro Islamic Liberation Front was in a sense treated with what's called a parity of esteem, which is a really important concept in peace processes. The idea that the asymmetrically weaker party is respected and given support to play a dynamic leading role in its own process and is not patronized.

I think this represents quite an important component of peace processes, which is often ignored – the notion of generosity. The President of Philippines, Aquino, did not need to be generous to the MILF, many people said. But he recognized that by being generous to the MILF, treating them with a parity of esteem would create a space in which they could reach a mutually acceptable outcome. I think that's a critical alchemy of a peace process.

Can you get the parties to agree to something that's in both of their interests?

The ICG, the International Contact Group started operating in about 2009. By 2012, a framework agreement was reached. And by 2014, a comprehensive peace agreement was reached through some 40-odd rounds of talks.

Our role was to be at the talks, to be sitting in the room, though not necessarily at the table where the parties were sitting. My two colleagues, Kristian Herbolzheimer and Cynthia Petrigh, who was then replaced by Emma Leslie. We were there to support the facilitator in providing advice to the parties.

For instance, on occasion the facilitator would say, we've got a problem around an issue, say, demobilization. Can you talk to the MILF about what they need? Or can you arrange a training for them on a particular technical issue? We would also occasionally drafted non-papers on critical issues. Now, a non-paper is something that has no status. The states were very reluctant to do this. Because if a government writes something, if a state writes something, it has a bit of authority and, and you can't just scrump it up and throw it away if it's useless. Whereas if an NGO writes a non-paper and no one likes it, they can all throw it away with no loss of face, but they can also gradually start to take ideas from it.

I recall on one occasion a dynamic that with hindsight is quite amusing – Kristian was based in Barcelona, and Emma was in the region at the talks that were taking place in Kuala Lumpur. On this occasion a number of issues were proving too hard to pin down and causing disagreement. Emma sent her notes to Kristian in Barcelona and went to bed. Kristian received them in the morning and whilst everyone in Kuala Lumpur was asleep it, he rewrote the notes and sent a paper back for the next morning that made sense of their discussion and blockages and led to a more productive discussion the following day. Such contributions were one small component in the parties having the space to talk to one another and really hash out critical issues.

Now you'll see there's only one woman in this photo, and it really speaks to the gender dynamic in peace processes. Someone missing from this photo is a wonderful woman called Miriam Coronel-Ferrer. Miriam was the negotiator for the Philippines government. She's actually the first woman to negotiate a peace agreement. Can you believe it? Formally, since people have been documenting peace processes since the Second World War, and since before that as well, it was a male dominated space. But what's very interesting was to see that with both the government and the MILF lots of their advisors were women. They really heeded the advice to bring women into the process.

I must admit, there are times when international mediators say to conflict parties: you need more women in the process. This was very interesting in Syria when the UN mediators were all men. But they'd be telling the parties, you need more women in your negotiations team! There's a certain irony in that.

But what was important is that behind this male-dominated process, you had the extraordinary activism of women's groups, caucusing, reflecting on what their communities needed, and actually engaging in the civic endeavour that creates the kind of social fabric that enables a formal negotiation to succeed. I think that the experience of the Philippines process shed a lot of light on the gender dynamics and the obstacles women face, but also the opportunities for civic engagement and the contribution women make.

It was a fascinating process of talks over a five or six year period of learning, and of the empowerment of the MILF to become a more effective interlocutor.

An agreement was reached in 2014. Since then, the critical thing has been the transition phase towards implementing that agreement.

And next year will be a critical year because there will be elections in the Bangsamoro region, the first fully open elections, that will elect a new government. And the Moro political parties are really going through a process of establishing their identity as political parties. That is far from easy. The process of moving from being an armed resistance movement to being a political movement, to being a political party, to being bureaucrats, running a political administrative entity is far from straightforward and needs a lot of assistance.

It brings me to one of the first key lessons in this, which I think is that we often look at the importance of reaching a peace agreement, focusing on the deal, but far too little attention is placed on the implementation of an agreement. And the implementation phase takes a long time.

The deal was 2014, but the implementation has been continuing for a decade. And actually the ICG became much less important after the deal. But at certain moments and recently has been one, when the parties have stumbled on certain obstacles in the implementation, they've come back to the ICG to get them involved in providing technical advice and spaces for constructive discussion.

One of the roles we've been playing recently is doing separate work with the government peace panel and with the MILF peace panel to help them envision what they need out of the next phase of the process before they come back together.

The whole question of implementation is crucial, recognizing that most peace processes fail within the first five years. Really investing adequately in the implementation and not thinking, oh, well we've got the deal now, we can bugger off to the next process, is I think, critical.

The exclusion of women is another critical lesson. There's a whole debate about UN Resolution 1325 on Women, Peace and Security, and it'll be the 25th anniversary next year, which is an important milestone. What's been learned is how little has been done to actually realize the full and equal participation of women in peace processes. There's been a trend in recent years to create several networks of women mediators, which is important. But quite often the idea is you have these networks of senior level women and the consideration is to parachute them into peace processes. It is highly problematic because you parachute people in to fail.

If you think that a woman can just turn up at a table and change it... actually where the really dynamic engagement of women in peace processes is, is not that that shouldn't happen, not that women shouldn't be at the table, but that on their own you set people up for failure. The really dynamic work is often happening in what women are doing at the community level where they are having to constantly mediate endless conflicts within the community. That's where much more support is needed. And this will percolate through to influence and provide access to, political processes.

The question of geopolitics is critical in this. The kind of hybrid mechanism about which I spoke, worked in the Philippines because although every context in the world has geopolitics, and the United States and China both have very particular interests in the Philippines, it wasn't the most geopolitically contested conflict. So, there was space for quite a creative hybrid mechanism to be established. I don't know that it would work everywhere, but it certainly worked in that context.

There were also a number of other lessons. I've touched on the way states and NGOs can work together. The NGOs could do a lot of the back channelling because we, as much as we don't want to, we can afford to be burnt in a way that states can't. If they get things wrong, it's bloody uncomfortable for them, damages their credibility. But if an NGO gets things wrong, it's unfortunate, but it isn't as critical. If a state gets something wrong, it can have much graver consequences on multiple levels.

So I think there's an interesting dynamic of how you get states and NGOs to work together in the interest of pushing a peace process forward.

Another critical role is how a mechanism like this, which is an external one, intersects with civil society in the context and to ensure that the voice of civil society is not squeezed out. There were tensions around this because a very rich and powerful civil society has grown up in the Philippines emanating from the movement to remove President Marcos in the 1980s, and lots of them weren't happy at the fact that this was an external group without local and national civil society being involved.

There was a lot of work done to create connections and the NGO participants in the ICG to be a little bit of a conduit for the voice of local and national civil society in the formal process.

A critical dimension in relation to the implementation question is how do you create a peace architecture and an infrastructure that covers the spectrum of challenges that you're going to find in the peace process?

In addition to the International Contact Group, you also had something called the Third Party Monitoring Mission, which was a mechanism to monitor the implementation of the peace agreement and to monitor the ceasefire. You had the Bangsamoro transitional authority to help put in place government structures. These are examples of the multiple different types of structures connecting with civil society, connecting with government structures that enable change to happen.

It's a complex process. It has to be choreographed. And in the Philippines, it went through a very difficult phase after President Aquino, when President Duterte was elected. You might remember the extraordinary scale of extra-judicial killing that happened under Duterte – who was from Mindanao, in fact.

But changes in the political climate of a country can have a very big impact on how a peace agreement is implemented. Gwen alluded to that in regard to the fact that an opponent of the peace agreement was elected after President Santos who had overseen the attainment of the peace agreement.

The final points in relation to lessons are the following:

One is around the culture you are creating and my colleague Emma Leslie made a wonderful observation about the importance of being tough on issues and soft on people. That's a really important lesson.

It's good to think about what that means in a peace process, where you're trying to support people who've been through traumatic experiences, to transform – but they're dealing with really tough issues. How do you help them in that process?

Diana mentioned the multiple paths idea in the Philippines, and I think it's a really important one. You might be familiar with people talking about multi-track diplomacy. My colleague Kristian would speak about the multiple paths to peace. People talk about track one, the formal processes, track one and a half, which is formal people in informal processes and track two, which is civil society processes. And in fact, there's a whole ... seven or nine track map. But actually the problem with tracks is they can be very linear, rigid and hierarchical, and peace processes are not linear and they're not rigid and they're messy. So this idea of multiple paths criss-crossing one another is very important.

In the Philippines they developed a notion of six paths to peace, which recognized the multiplicity of factors that have to interweave to enable peace to get traction.

And then really important in this is the recognition that you have a transition phase. You might get an agreement that peace doesn't come overnight. And that's really where you need to invest, where you are looking at how, as I said earlier, a group like the Moro Islamic Liberation Front does transform into different type of actor so that it can be a political player. One of the lessons I learned from study visits we did to Northern Ireland was the necessity of moving from violence to politics as a way to resolve conflict. I think that's a really important framing to keep in mind. And that's what groups like the MILF, like the FARC, had to go through, to move from violence to politics as a way of achieving political ends.

I think that's enough. Thank you.

Questions to Jonathan Cohen

Q: What about opportunism if things change and there's a moment of opportunity and you've got structures and you've got processes [going on...].

A: It's a great question. It gives me an opportunity to mention something that a number of my colleagues would shoot me for not having mentioned. We talk an awful lot about adaptive peace-building, that you have to be able to adapt to the changing scenarios because conflict is fluid, it changes. What you're doing as a peace-building actor has to be able to adapt to those changes. And the critical one is, are you able to seize moments of change that require resources? It requires an ability on the part of an NGO to turn around to a donor and say, we weren't going to do that, but actually the situation's changed. We now need to do that. Sometimes it's absurd the responses you get. You know, sorry, financial year ends next month, you can't do that. I think it also requires political actors to have the confidence to be able to respond.

And there's the importance of civil society, and the way Gwen spoke about demonstrated that as being absolutely fundamental to peace processes. But we mustn't forget the importance of leaders. And their ability to lead. Gwen could have told a lot of stories about President Santos, who's a complex figure, but who did lead and who was prepared to make compromises. Compromise is often a very dirty word in conflicts. If you can't make compromises, what are you going to achieve? It's about seizing opportunities, both at the societal level and at the political level; you need confidence and you actually need conviction to do that. One of the things that feeds confidence and feeds conviction is preparation. It's people having thought through the hard issues in advance so that when things change, they can act quickly.

Q: What role has secrecy got in success? Secrecy, confidentiality, call it what you want.

A: It's sensitive because on the one hand there's an absolutely legitimate demand for openness and transparency, and societies want to know what's being negotiated in their name. But on the other hand, it can be important that you don't let the cat out of the bag too soon because it can undermine the credibility of a compromise that's going to be made. So it's a very fine line that has to be trod.

Q: I've been doing a little bit of self-reflection during this afternoon's talks and thinking we are people who (probably all of us) hold quite strong opinions about various things. How do we avoid becoming parties to conflict ourselves while still persuading the other? And what can you learn from your sort of experiences?

A: Well, what are you implying?

Q: Think self-reflection, having peer groups with whom you can have safe conversations in which you can be challenged to ask yourself about your motivations, your values, why you're doing it.

A: Listening...

Q: Yes.

A: Interestingly enough, I mentioned this to colleagues the other day. I was listening to a podcast in which someone was talking about the importance of broadcasting, but also the importance of broad listening. And I really like that notion of broad listening to be able to listen beyond your comfort zone. So I mentioned it earlier today, I think the combination of patience and impatience is really critical. Because when you do this work, you do need to be patient, both with yourself and with other people. And you have to learn to be able to hold the discomfort of positions you find abhorrent. Even on a personal level, on a number of occasions I've had to shake hands with people who have perpetrated appalling things.

You recognize that actually there's a purpose to doing this, and you have to sit with discomfort, but you also have to be impatient. Because if you don't keep pushing, you'd be better giving up.

Q: As we move towards evaluating our day, and perhaps we won't have time for that? perhaps over a beer ? do you have any couple of sentences about how you evaluate, either you or the community evaluates, what you do?

A: It's a really important question because one of the problems we face is generating evidence, documenting evidence, and telling the story of what works, in order to demonstrate the impact of what we do. Because all too often you're having to convince the donors that you're having an impact. And one of the things that we've realized is we are not nearly good enough at telling the story.

There's an obsession with data, and actually it's the stories, the personal stories that are important.

We've started to use a methodology called *outcome harvesting* in recent years, which is about — and it sounds a bit technical maybe — but it's been an incredibly powerful way of getting our colleagues who are working across multiple regions to think about the stories of change they're observing, and to think about their contribution to those stories of change, and think about what the outcome is, and to harvest the multiple contributions that have been made.

The way we do that is through discussion sessions with teams where they talk about the progress towards change. In fact, a few months back we published a report on it. It's really interesting. It gets a bit technical, but I think it's a brilliant articulation of how you can evaluate in a much more sophisticated way.

Fundamentally what our whole community has to do is to be good at telling the story of how change happens, to convince publics, to convince donors, to convince politicians, that there are different ways to move towards the abolition of war.

I'd just like to add to that very briefly. I mean, I think you are in a role; you can tell I'm not a kind of 'anything goes' person. I've got very definite views, but when I've got a job and I'm in that job. Yeah. And it doesn't even feel tempting to be the person I could be. Because this is what I've got to do. This is my job and I actually disagree about the facilitating and the mediating. I think a good mediator is a facilitator for other people to talk to each other and come to a conclusion.

Diana Francis – closing

Thank you. Thank you.
Thank you all. We've got five minutes.
If you have a 'one word evaluation', please raise your hand.

"Spiriting"

Thank you. Extraordinarily good.
Two words now.

Any other 'just one word' thoughts on 'Spiriting'

I like that. Insightful. Yes. Yes.

Useful, useful. Hooray,

'*Enlarging'.*

Yes. Me too. Yeah.

Well, I, feel hugely grateful to loads of people.
So I don't forget them.
I thank the organizers because I know how much work they've put in on top of that.

David Collins – Many thanks to Olivier Stockman and Christine Edzard, who run this establishment in which people pay what they can afford, which is completely wonderful. Nobody is excluded and that's how everything works here. It has been great. Roger has absolutely achieved miracles in that box at the back there..

Diana – I thank Olivier and Christine at Sands.
Those speakers ... obviously, thank you very much. All those of you who've spoken.
I think we've all learned a lot. Well, thank you very much all of you for being really great with attention and questions and time keeping and everything else and just being here. It's been great to have you.
So thanks to everybody!